FERRARI

PROJECT EDITOR
Valeria Manferto De Fabianis

EDITORIAL STAFF
Giorgia Raineri

EDITORIAL COORDINATION
Laura Accomazzo

GRAPHIC DESIGN
Maria Cucchi

FERRARI

An Italian Legend

TEXT BY ROBERTO BONETTO

METRO BOOKS
New York

Contents

Origin of a Myth	page 12		The 1980s: An Increasing Decade	page 144
1947: The Birth of a Legend	page 28		Ferrari Mondial 8	page 146
Auto Avio Constructions 815	page 30		Ferrari Testarossa	page 150
Ferrari 166	page 34		Ferrari 288 GTO	page 156
Ferrari 342 America	page 42		Ferrari F40	page 160
Ferrari 212 Export	page 46		Ferrari 348 TB/TS	page 168
The 1950s: The Roaring Years	page 54		The 1990s: New Ideas among the GTs	page 176
Ferrari 375 America	page 56		Ferrari 456 GT	page 178
Ferrari 250 GT California	page 68		Ferrari F355	page 182
The 1960s: Decisive Years also for Cars	page 78		Ferrari 512 M	page 188
Ferrari 250 GT SWB	page 80		Ferrari F50	page 192
Ferrari 250 GTO	page 88		Ferrari 550 Maranello	page 202
Ferrari 275 GTB	page 92		Ferrari 360 Modena	page 206
Ferrari 250/330 Le Mans	page 102		The 2000s: The Era of Supercars	page 214
Ferrari 330 GT 2+2	page 110		Ferrari 550 Barchetta Pininfarina	page 216
Ferrari Dino 206	page 116		Ferrari Enzo	page 220
Ferrari 365 GT 2+2	page 122		Ferrari F430	page 232
Ferrari 365 GTB4 Daytona	page 126		Ferrari 612 Scaglietti	page 240
The 1970s: Hope Constrained by Austerity	page 132		Ferrari 458 Italia	page 244
Ferrari 308 GTB	page 134		Ferrari California	page 250
Ferrari 512 BB	page 138		Ferrari 599 GTO	page 258
			Ferrari Four	page 262
			Author's biography - Index	page 268

3 Details of the 330 TRI/LM's nose, winner of the Le Mans in 1962. A similar auto was recently sold at an auction for almost 7 million euros, the highest price ever paid for a Ferrari.

4-5 The California is one of the most beautiful Spiders ever. Commissioned by Ferrari himself in 1957 following Chinetti's advice, 107 units were masterfully built by Franco Scaglietti for the sportier clients thirsting for racing thrills.

6-7 Built in 1995, the F50 was designed for racing and became an incomparable Grand Tourer. Made of composite materials, 349 samples were produced following the Formula One technology, with a V12 engine of 286.79 cu. in. (4.7 liters) and 520 hp.

8-9 The Enzo of 2002 exhibited a special F1 line with a V12 engine of 366.12 cu. in. (6 liters) with 660 hp. It was the synthesis of technological mechanics, aerodynamics and electronics. A total of 399 models of this "integrated system" were made and reaped great success worldwide.

10-11 The "faired-in" tail for the fuel mouth and the driver's tiny roll bar exemplify one of the typical style lines of the Ferrari sports cars, especially the 315 S of 1957, winner of the last Mille Miglia race.

Before May 25, 1947 – the year in which the Scuderia Ferrari, with its prancing horse symbol inherited from World War I pilot Francesco Baracca, won the Roman Grand Prix with a new car, Sport 1500 – very few knew about this tiny factory that had survived World War II thanks to military supplies, grinders and lathes. Finally in 1947, its founder, Enzo Ferrari, Alfa Romeo driver from 1924 to 1929 and then manager of his own sports division, could return to cultivating his dream: racing cars.

The first was built by Gioacchino Colombo, a technician he met in the 1930s at the Alfa Races, who proposed an almost insane idea: a car intended first for racing, then for road-legal speed touring, driven by 12 cylinders – a daring project that would have turned into the most outstanding legend in the history of automobiles.

Then the company, which until 1940 could count on 40 employees, saw the arrival of a new project designer, Giuseppe Busso, who tried to set up some kind of technical system. But despite his abilities as a calculator of automobile mechanics, he could not deal with the atmosphere, as he confirmed in his memoirs: "Living in Maranello in mid-1946 was not simple, with the rationing of fuel and electric energy, and difficulty in finding bread and pasta. Despite all this, [Ferrari] stood out as the charismatic and absolute leader. When I left Maranello or rather, escaped from Maranello at the end of 1947 to respond to the providential allure of the Alfa, I would never have imagined that following this event, such affection and gratitude for the 'Commendatore' (an honor given by the Italian government in 1923) would mature within me."

With his usual skills and stubbornness, Ferrari fulfilled his dream of building a car of his own that bore his name. Finally, on May 11, 1947, the 12-cylinder Spirit 125 was presented on the Piacenza racing circuit.

12-13 Enzo Ferrari is seen here at the Monza Race Circuit on June 3, 1924. This was the year in which the P2 took command (6 cylinders, 122.04 cu. in. – 2 liters) with 140 hp and 139.5 mph (225 km/h); the Alfa driver did not compete in the Grand Prix that year due to a serious nervous breakdown.

But it was not an excellent debut and the car, driven by trusted driver Franco Cortese, dropped out only three laps from the end of the race. Two weeks later, Ferrari, his 125 S and Franco Cortese showed up again at the Roman Grand Prix and determined the history of the Prancing Horse with its first important victory. It was just the beginning of an infinite legend. The 12-cylinder engine designed by Colombo became a symbol for the new company, which relocated from Modena to Maranello (16 km south of Modena) in 1943. From then on, the Prancing Horse icon was mounted on all the racing and road-legal touring sports cars.

The elegance of the 12 cylinders and the mastery of the Pininfarina, Vignale and Touring bodyworks on top of such prestigious mechanics resulted in Ferrari's immediate leadership: renowned drivers, important top managers and rich Americans became precious clients of the newborn factory. Only two cars were produced in 1947, five the year after and 113 in 1957. Even young Gianni Agnelli had a car built – a special blue-green 166 MM Touring Barchetta with a white leather interior. Sporting triumphs abounded, from the 1948 Mille Miglia to the 24 Hours of Le Mans. But Ferrari cultivated more ambitious goals, sought new fame and wanted to beat the queen of Formula One, the Alfa Romeo 158 designed before the war precisely in his own factory. The Alfa-Ferrari battle enlivened the entire two years of sports from 1950 to 1951, while Maranello produced the very classy Gran Turismo, precious models like the 212 Inter and the 340 America, so much desired by the "commendatore" and his U.S. agent, Luigi Chinetti. These cars were not easy to tame but were fascinating due to those powerful 12 cylinders under their hoods and because they were so challenging to drive.

14-15 The 66 SC of 1947 was one of the first Ferrari racecars that later was transformed into a Grand Tourer. This strange prewar type of chassis was driven by Tazio Nuvolari in the Mille Miglia of 1947.

Ferrari turned up at the new 1952–1953 World Championships and won all there was to win with his single-seater 4-cylinder 500. His cars took absolute command in Europe, and even competed in Indianapolis, though unsuccessfully.

The numerous wins in the most classic European races were crucial to sustain even the most meager production: in 1950 only 26 cars were produced in Maranello; this rose to 306 in 1960 and reached 1,000 within the next 10 years.

1954 was a normal year for Ferrari: the Mercedes returned to Formula One and took command for two years. But Ferrari insisted on his racing cars, which continued to nurture the Prancing Horse myth the world over; he could count on a specialized handcrafted production of utmost quality, but with only 61 cars. Then there were the Grand Touring models for the American market, such as the 375 or the 410 Superfast, and the first series of the 250 GT, all branded Pininfarina (by then the official chassis designer of the house).

In 1957, the new challenge in Formula One was launched by the Maserati 250F in the person of four-time world champion Juan Manuel Fangio. The two young Ferrari drivers, Mike Hawthorn and Peter Collins, battled to the end but the Argentine wizard, Fangio, was really superior and retired from the scene at the age of 47 with five world titles. 1958 once again started off with the theoretical supremacy of Ferrari on the Formula One horizon. So in 1966, the British automakers Cooper and Lotus, with their evolved, lightweight, rear-engine single-seaters, traced new technological paths also in the "lower" ranges. They did this even though under the flag of the newborn Dino series, there were no 12-cylinder engines but their derivatives, the V6s of 122.04 or 152.55 cu. in. (2 or 2.5 liters), installed at the rear, the outcome of a new financial agreement with Fiat.

The big 12 cylinders remained forever a classic example of prestige and profits, which Ferrari certainly had no intention of renouncing. In 1965 the company produced 740 autos – quite an important figure for the tiny Maranello factory, where cars were personally fetched by their owners, mainly international celebrities and crowned heads, from the Shah of Persia to Gary Cooper, from the King of Sweden to the Princess of Belgium. In 1957 the Pininfarina series began, though timidly, with the mass production of the 250 GT, which won many races. In 1959, the 250 GT excelled, together with the Berlinetta sedan designed by Pininfarina and built by Scaglietti, and became a constant in the Maranello production, still rich in custom-built series. At the onset of the '60s, the 250 GT was still in vogue and the new GT 2+2 further widened the range of Ferrari customers with production now reaching 601 cars yearly. Also, in Bologna the "commendatore" was awarded an ad honorem degree in engineering, a distinction he always took pride in.

Ferrari prestige was at its peak with its countless championship victories. Even so, at the end of 1961, the company suffered a harsh blow when eight of its top managers left Maranello for other shores. But this engineer had overcome bigger trials and went ahead unwaveringly along his path. Simultaneously with sportive activities, the production of the 250 Berlinetta road model continued, enriched with accessories that were crucial to a modern Grand Tourer: steel chassis (instead of aluminum), bumpers, winding panes and leather interiors. Ferrari had to acknowledge English superiority in Formula One but at the same time produced one of his most prestigious, legendary cars, the 250 GTO (Grand Touring Homologated), a winner in both sports car and road car races (three world titles). A priceless jewel in auctions, the car today is the epitome of the team's experience in extreme sports competitions. The initial design by Giotto Bizzarrini was well accomplished by Mauro Forghieri, a 26-year-old engineer who became famous. 1963 witnessed a firm resurgence of sports activities, in Formula One, the Constructors' Trophy for GT and Prototypes. The production's gems were the 250 GTOs and especially the Luxury, which replaced the "short wheelbase" Berlinetta; however, it was not as successful. 1964 saw the revival of racing activities in Formula One (the World Championship won by John Surtees) and in the Sport category, with the 250 LM, also a road car, 34 of which were produced in two years. But there also was another prestigious Berlinetta, ever more road-going, the 275 GTB of 200.44 cu. in. (3,286 cc), with classic mechanics and 280 hp, hitting a top speed of 159.96 mph (258 km/h). Designed by Pininfarina, produced (about 500 units up to 1968) by Scaglietti.

17 Enzo Ferrari, already at the peak of his popularity, is shown at the wheel of one of his Sport models of 1964. That year proved to be fulfilling in terms of sports and commercial success.

18-19 The "275 Daytona" models attracted attention, especially in the endurance races, due to their speed and sturdiness. Their "career" began in 1968 in Le Mans at Chinetti's request and the car finished fifth overall at the 24 Hours of 1979. In 1971, the company produced 15 Daytonas in aluminum and fiberglass panels.

1967: in the Sport category, the gigantic Ford battled with the little Ferrari. Now Maranello won, but Ford captured the more prestigious title of the 24 Hours of Le Mans. In the market, the tiny Ferrari-Dino with 6 cylinders gained many fans, but the 12-cylinders, such as the 365 GT 2+2 and rear-engine 365 P, also demonstrated the house's upper-class technical level. Formula One in 1968 was anything but positive, but at least the refined, much appreciated, classic and astounding 365 GTB/4 Daytona came to life: it was a Pininfarina design with 352 hp that reached 280 km/h (174 mph).

1969 came up with a decisive novelty: Ferrari merged with Fiat, which now owned 50 percent. This sports year, however, was one of the worst for Maranello. The Grand Touring models highlighted the 6-cylinder Dino, which increased its engine displacement, now at 147.55 cu. in. (2,419 cc), and output, going from 180 to 195 hp. Then came the more powerful 12 cylinders, such as the 365 Coupe and Spider that flanked the Daytona. In 1970 the Formula One season opened with the 312 B, which was theoretically unbeatable, its 12 Boxer cylinders delivering 460 hp (on evolving, it would have lasted 11 years). But the Lotus won the World Title. In the "Sport Prototypes" championship, the Porsche was unbeatable. Then the fascinating 365 GTB 12 cylinders, nicknamed the "hunchback," came up. Still in 1971, few titles were won in both Formula One and the Sport category, where the Porsche 917 continued

to reign. Among the GTs, the BB prototype (365 GT/4 BB) was produced successfully for many years, with a rear Boxer engine – a real record for Maranello.

In 1972, Formula 1 gave scarce satisfaction and the 312 B2 won only the Nürburgring GP. In that year there were still great results in the Sport category where the 312 PB was unrivaled. The GT group advertised the 365 GT/4 2+2, not the utmost in beauty but functional and very popular. 1973 gave no satisfaction in racing; the more interesting feature was the pro-duction of the 365 GT/4, also known as the BB, with an output of 380 hp and 300 km/h (186 mph), which set a new standard for the supersport cars of Maranel-lo. Also the tiny Dino underwent some changes, be-coming a V8 in the four-seater coupe version (Bertone body) or two-seater *Berlinetta* (Pininfarina).

1975 was a magical year for the Prancing Horse, which won the Formula One World Championship with Niki Lauda, Clay Regazzoni and the 312 T. The 308 GTB also made its debut, an 8-cylinder; compact and very fast Berlinetta, also made its debut; it was the forerunner of a new family of sports cars. In 1976 Ferrari lost the F1 World Championship, which it seemed to hold in its hands up to the last minute of the Japan Grand Prix. The production's strong points were still the sporty BB and the stately GTA 400, very popular especially in the U.S.A. Having recovered from the Nürburgring fire accident, Lauda with his 312 T2 regained his supremacy, bagging three Grand Prix and the 1977 World Championship.

1979 was a glorious year for the 312 T4 with which Jody Scheckter became world champion. In 1980, the new T5 did not win any race. A new world title was won by the Grand Touring four-seaters on a "rear engine" with the 183.06 cu. in. (3-liter) V8 of 215 hp.

1981: The entry of the Turbo engines upset the Formula One. Maranello's queen of production, the 500 BB, was turbocharged and delivered 340 hp. In 1982, Ferrari had all it needed to win the Formula One: the 126 C2 and two young and aggressive drivers, Gilles Villeneuve and Didier Pironi, with an excellent 6 turbo cylinders (600 hp). The season, however, ended badly. Even in production the turbo overpowered the "small" 208, supercharged up to 220 hp, whereas the V8-122 cu. in. (2,000 cc) of the World Championship was equipped with the V8 of 32 valves, with 240 hp. In the 1984 production (2,842 cars), Ferrari could boast of top-of-the-line examples such as the 288 GTO twin-turbo with 400 hp, an extraordinary Berlinetta; it was accompanied by the Testarossa with 390 hp for its 12 Boxer cylinders. In 1986, Ferrari in Formula One still placed its bet on the turbo and improved its aerodynamics to 212.04 mph (342 km/h!), but could not fend off Prost's McLaren-Porsche. The turbo also took command in the GTB V6, 2 liters of 254 hp.

In 1987, the Ferrari team hired John Barnard as technical director of the F1-87; its single-seater was competitive but not always reliable, and won in two Grand Prix with Gerhard Berger (fifth in the World Championship). 1987 also marked the 40th anniversary of the company's founding; it celebrated the event in the best way with the prestigious, "extreme" F40, an epoch-making event with mechanics, design and exemplary performance, thanks to the 8-cylinder twin-turbo of 478 hp and advanced aerodynamics (grand rear aileron) delivering a top speed of 200.88 mph (324 km/h).

1988 was a year of mourning following the death of Enzo Ferrari, age 90, on August 14. Ferrari won the Italian Grand Prix, though Gerhard Berger and Michele Alboreto took third and fifth in the World Championship. 1989 saw the birth of the F1-89, with an aspirated V12, five valves per cylinder, 600-650 hp, innovative aerodynamics and above all a revolutionary 7-speed semiautomatic transmission speeds controlled by levers at the wheel, later introduced in the GT series. The new Ferrari member, Nigel Mansell, won the first Grand Prix in Brazil and then in Hungary, but in the end made only fourth place in the World Championship. Always regarding the turbo, the 348 TB/TS with 300 hp appeared in the market and at the Motor Show, and Pininfarina's Mythos concept made its debut.

1990 was a fiery year in Formula One between Alain Prost (Ferrari) and Ayrton Senna (McLaren-Honda), which ended only at the conclusion with a violent contact between the two and with Senna winning the title. Senna and his McLaren-Honda took command also in 1991, but this time battled with the Williams-Renault instead of the Ferrari of Prost, who was fired due to some of his anti-Maranello declarations. In the 1992 production, the evolution of the Testarossa admiral stood out, reaching a level of 428 hp with catalyzed exhaust pipes. With disappointing results in F1 still in 1992, Maranello underwent a production remake with the traditional 456 with 12 front mounted cylinders of 442 hp and variable calibration of suspensions, exceeding the 186 mph (300 km/h) mark.

1995: the 12-cylinder engine made its last Formula One race, winning only one Grand Prix with Jean Alesi. The team played its trump card with the exclusive supercar, the F50 Berlinetta — practically a F1 roadster, which celebrated the brand's 50th anniversary ahead of time. Only 359 buyers sought prototypes of the car, which were built with a V12 of 286.79 cu. in. (4.7 liters) and 520 hp, an exceptional elasticity and speed of 201.5 mph (325 km/h). The "tiny" 355, instead, then became a true "total" Spider with electric convertible top.

20 21 Ferrari described the 512 T4 as the ugliest F1 racecar Maranello ever produced, but thanks to new aerodynamics it grabbed the 1974 Constructors' and Drivers' World Titles with Jody Scheckter (3 G.Prix), sustained also by Gilles Villeneuve (4 G.Prix). The lines were "strange" but valid: a narrow body shell and a pointed nose with greater air flows due to the flat underbody's ground effect. Also, the chassis with broad front and rear flaps contributed to the effectiveness of the "unusual" aerodynamics that counted on the greater 515 hp output of its Boxer engine.

21 top 1990 was the year that saw the battle between Alain Prost (Ferrari) and Ayrton Senna (McLaren) who won the World Championship. The photo was shot at the Monza Grand Prix where the Ferrari F641 with its 680 hp was the best single-seater and practically monopolized the public's attention.

1996: Twice world champion Michael Schumacher, hired at a costly price (around 40 billion lire yearly), began his outstanding odyssey, which would have crowned him with five world titles with the Prancing Horse. Production took an important leap forward: the 550 was produced in Maranello in compliance with all the Ferrari rules, 12 front cylinders with 485 hp, gears and rear-wheel drive and excellent drivability. 1999: The novelty in production was that the F355 F1 had electronic gears derived from the F1. 1997: Mika Häkkinen with his McLaren-Mercedes appeared on the scene, and for two years took the title away from Schumacher and the Ferrari 310 B.

1999 saw the birth of the 360 Modena, a "tiny" innovation in aluminum which, with its 400 hp and V8, was a true leader on the road. Finally in 2000, the group triumphed again with its very advanced F1 model, much narrower, very much lighter and more powerful (770 hp). The battle between McLaren-Mercedes and Häkkinen still continued, but then Schumacher triumphed with nine victories, bringing the Constructors' title also back to Maranello. Two interesting Spiders were produced, the 360 and the 500 Barchetta with the construction of only 448 prototypes.

In 2001, in Formula One, the Prancing Horse's supremacy became even more evident. It won both titles (with Schumacher's nine victories). The results were excellent also in terms of production: the 550 Maranello became the 575 M (515 hp) with manual progressive gearbox. And not only this: here was another up-market car, the Enzo, an extreme roadster with all the Formula One innovations and solutions: carbon steel body, 12 cylinders of 660 hp, 6 gears applied with levers at the wheel, and exceptional stability. 2003 was a triumphal season for the Ferrari in Formula One, with Schumacher winning his sixth world title. The new F2003-GA (850 hp) of the F1 evolved, but the world championship was more difficult than foreseen; in the end, however, Schumacher overtook Kimi Räikkönen's McLaren-Mercedes. The 612 Scaglietti was then unveiled – the first all-aluminum 12-cylinder Ferrari with 540 hp, sufficient to reach 195.3 mph (315 km/h).

2005 was an unfortunate season: the title went to Fernando Alonso on a Renault, whereas the Prancing Horse recouped by winning the FIA GT world title with the 550 Maranello. The fascinating Superamerica made its comeback with an electric convertible top. The hope for 2006 was to grab the title from Alonso's Renault, but things ended differently. A record was set in production, however: 2,800 employees with 5,671 automobiles (4.8 percent more than in 2005). Another highlight was the presentation of the new 599 GTB Fiorano, Berlinetta 366 cu. in. (6,000 cc) which Maranello nicknamed "the prettiest of all," also with a superior output (620 hp).

In 2007 after Schumacher stopped racing, the team began anew with Räikkönen, who won the world title (by just one point!) – a victory was celebrated with a special series of 60 Ferrari cars in different colors. 2008 started under a lucky star: Felipe Massa could have won the title in Brazil, but in the last race Lewis Hamilton with his McLaren-Mercedes won the Pilots' title. Ferrari at least won the Constructors' title. Then came the exclusive Spider, the new California, a 2+2 Spider with metallic modular top, classical drive train, 8 cylinders of 460 hp, direct injection, 7-speed transmission on the rear axle, and top speed of 192.2 mph (310 km/h) – another signature car for the diehard Ferrari fans.

2009 was the year of the new Formula One, with rules that paid special attention to and favored new teams like those of the BAR, the former Honda, with aerodynamics so effective that they beat even the stronger makes. It was, however, an important year for Ferrari production, since two models were built: the California Spider and the 458 Italia, a great, compact 8-cylinder that replaced the obsolete F430 of 2004.

The 2010 range was the foundation for the future Ferrari, in a year that, for once, could have been Alonso's and Ferrari's big chance. In the end, however, the Red Bull-Renault of the upcoming star, Sebastian Vettel, won the title in quite an action-packed atmosphere.

23 Pit stops for fuel top-ups and tire changing are among the most crucial moments of current Grand Prix races and may be decisive in winning the races. The stop and restart is estimated at about 25 seconds between the stop and go. This shot taken during the GP 2010 shows the n.1 car of Fernando Alonso.

24-25 Born to win the first Grand Touring of 1962, the 250 GTO was conceived by Engineer Giotto Bizzarrini, who designed an extreme chassis of such a harsh beauty that it conquered all the sports enthusiasts. Only 36 samples were built, and it achieved an impressive sports curriculum of three world titles and more than 200 wins the world over.

26-27 Another step forward for the compact Ferraris: 430 stood for engine displacement (262 cu. in. – 4.3 liters); it was the successor of the 360 Modena, and had a very powerful V8 (460 hp) and maximum aerodynamics with ground effect. In 2005, it was placed alongside the Spider version.

1947:

The Birth of a Legend

IN ITALY, PROSTRATED BY WORLD WAR II, THE FACTORIES AND ENGINEERS STARTED WORKING AGAIN FOR THE AUTO-MOBILE INDUSTRY. THOUGH BATTERED BY WORLD EVENTS, THE MOST EFFICIENT COMPANIES EMERGED, SUCH AS FIAT AND THEN LANCIA AND ALFA ROMEO, WHICH IN 1947 PRODUCED ABOUT 44,000 CARS — MOSTLY FIAT 500/TOPOLINO, THEN AL-SO SOME LANCIA AND THE ALFA WITH THE SPORTY BERLINA AND THE POSH 2500. THE ITALIANS WERE AMONG THE FIRST TO ROLL UP THEIR SLEEVES. IN TURIN, THE CISITALIA COMPANY OWNED BY THE INDUSTRIALIST PIERO DUSIO ESTABLISHED A PRESTIGIOUS FACTORY FOR SPORTS CARS. BUT ALSO A DARING MANAGER, ENZO FERRARI, THEN SPORTS DIRECTOR OF THE ALFA RACING DIVISION, WAS BUILDING THE FIRST CAR BEARING HIS NAME. TO DESIGN IT, HE RECRUITED GIOACCHINO COLOMBO, WITH WHOM HE HAD ALREADY BUILT THE FAMOUS "ALFETTA" 158 DURING THE WAR. SO THE FIRST 12-CYLIN-DER ENGINE WAS DESIGNED (IN 1945) AND BUILT (ON SEPTEMBER 26, 1946), SETTING THE FOUNDATION FOR THE MARANELLO PRODUCTION. THIS SAW THE BIRTH OF THE 125 S, THE VERY FIRST REAL FERRARI, ON MARCH 12, 1947. THE "COMMENDATORE" HIMSELF LAUNCHED IT IN THE WORK YARDS OF MARANELLO. TWO MONTHS LATER ON MAY 11, FRAN-CO CORTESE DEBUTED WITH IT ON THE PIACENZA CIRCUIT. IT TOOK THE LEAD BUT DROPPED OUT TWO LAPS FROM THE END OF THE RACE. IN JUST TWO WEEKS, ON MAY 25, FRANCO CORTESE AND THE 125 S WON THE ROMAN GRAND PRIX. THE 125 S ALSO RAN IN THE FIRST POSTWAR MILLE MIGLIA ON JUNE 21, BUT WITHDREW FROM THE RACE. THE 125 S MADE GOOD PROGRESS IN 1948 AND 1949, WITH THE FERRARIS ALWAYS IN THE LEADING POSITIONS. IN 1947 ONLY THREE CARS WERE BUILT IN MARANELLO, WHICH HAD 140 EMPLOYEES. IN 1948 AT LEAST SIX FERRARIS TOOK PART IN THE MILLE MIGLIA, THE MOST IMPORTANT RACE OF THE TIME, AND THE 166 MM DRIVEN BY CLEMENTE BIONDETTI WITH GIUSEPPE NAVONE WON THE RACE. ALSO IN 1948, "MASTER" TAZIO NUVOLARI RAN HIS LAST MILLE MIGLIA IN A FERRARI THAT TOOK COMMAND, UP TO THE MOMENT WHEN MECHANICAL PROBLEMS FORCED HIM TO WITHDRAW. IN 1948 THE MARANELLO FACTORY WAS COMPLETED, AND IN 1949 THE SITUATION IMPROVED GREATLY: THERE WERE NOW 260 EMPLOYEES WHO BUILT A GOOD 21 CARS. THE NEW "BARCHETTA" 166 MM WON THE MILLE MIGLIA WITH GREAT EASE, THEN THE TOUR OF SICILY AND ABOVE ALL, THE 24 HOURS OF LE MANS, FUNDAMENTAL IN AFFIRMING THE PRANCING HORSE'S APPROVAL ABROAD, RUNNING 51 RACES AND WINNING 32. THE 125 GPC FORMULA 1 ALSO MADE ITS DEBUT WHILE THE REVOLUTIONARY 275 G.P. WAS STILL IN DEVELOPMENT WITHOUT A COMPRESSOR, IT WOULD LATER CHANGE THE GRAND PRIX RACES. THE REAL INDUSTRIAL PRO-DUCTION WOULD BEGIN IN THE 1950S.

Auto Avio Constructions 815

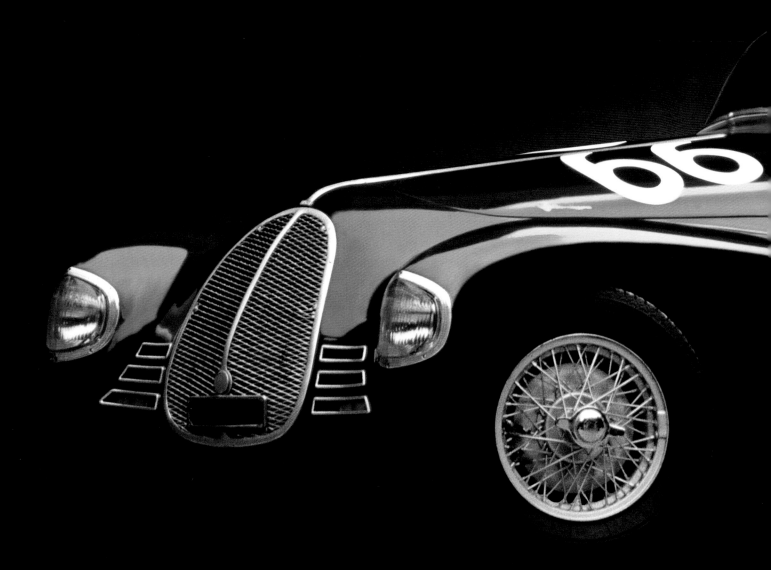

Auto Avio Constructions

With the war right at the doorstep, 1939 was certainly not an inviting year for the manufacture of new automobiles, especially racecars. But this was no deterrent for a man like Enzo Ferrari, a protagonist even when he was not in the limelight: for 10 years he and his team had managed the racing activities of the Alfa Romeo. The company said "enough" and withdrew since it had to face issues other than racing, and fired the "*commendatore*" and his highly acclaimed sports division. Ferrari had to think ahead about a way of constructing and he already was planning to build his very own automobile, bearing his own name. In spite of the noncompetition agreements signed with Alfa that prohibited him from doing so, he started working on a new motor. In Italy the situation was dramatic, to say the least: everyone was working primarily for the military and manufacturing thousands of automobiles as the specter of war increasingly loomed. But Ferrari, still burning with racing fever, was determined to find the necessary capital to build the car he had in mind. He looked for financial backers and some came to his aid: Alberto Ascari (son of one of the great champions of the 1920s, rival of the Campari, Borzacchini and also of Enzo Ferrari) and Count Lotario Rangoni Machiavelli, who wanted to run the 1940 Mille Miglia race with cars built at the Ferrari workshops. Prodded by the "commendatore," Engineers Alberto Massimino and Vittorio Bellentani, the brilliant Modena mechanics of the division, managed to make and prepare a small series of sports cars for the race in just four months. It seems that Ascari paid 20,000 lire for it. The Brescia race was held on a closed circuit passing through Cremona and Mantova, given the 1940 atmosphere that starkly contrasted with such events, and consisted of 102.3 miles (165 km) to be run through nine times for a total of 920.7 miles (1482 km). Europe was already at war, but some of the 75 participants came from Germany. For the two 815 cars (alias Ferrari) the Grand Prix of Brescia-Mille Miglia was a failure: they left on Sunday, April 28 at 4 a.m. and Ascari dropped out of the race at the first lap, while Rangoni continued through eight of the nine laps required. After two months, on June 10, Italy entered the hotbed of the war. The two 815 cars went

their own ways: on August 11, 1947, Ascari's car competed in the Pescara Circuit, side by side with the first "real" Ferrari, the 12-cylinder 125.

Not much could be expected in times when all was scarce, and the 815 could only make use of the design skills of two technicians and the mechanics of the already existing Alfa Corse. It was thus a beautiful car, though it necessarily had to make the best out of the materials available: this regarded the chassis which utilized components of the Fiat 508 C, adapted to the whims of the "*commendatore*," with spars (perforated) and reinforcing crosspieces, lightened as much as possible, and 8 cylinders shifted towards the center. The rest of the car also came from the 508 C. The chassis weighed 1,177 lbs. (535 kg), the complete car, 1,375 lbs. (625 kg). The 8-cylinder engine was a noteworthy example of a do-it-yourself spirit: the Ferrari cast a new monobloc in light alloy with drive shaft on five supports. As to the cylinder head, in order to save time, design and money, an original though somewhat empirical solution was found: two cylinder heads, always of the 508 C, joined together, with the 508's 4-speed gearbox. The very traditional suspensions were quadrilateral in front, with a stiff bridge with leaf springs at the rear-wheel, recalibrated for this new usage.

The lightweight alloy body was designed at the Touring, which was already working with the Ferrari Team. What resulted was a wonderful Spider, compact, and also designed for reproduction in small series. It was about 11.48 ft. (3.5 m) long, a typical Italian open-car model, with very prominent fenders and a longitudinal faired-in element connecting them. It had a flowing, pleasant line, which endowed dynamism and personality to the sides. Since the principal, Carlo Felice Bianchi Anderloni, was an army man, his father and founder, Felice, supervised the construction of the two cars. After the Mille Miglia, the 815 cars disappeared since they passed through the hands of different owners. But as mentioned, Ascari's car was seen on the Pescara race circuit, together with the first, real Ferrari 125. From 1975 onward, the Righini family from Emilia took possession of an 815 (perhaps Ascari's).

30-31 Designed and built at the Touring facilities in just four months, the 815 models bore carried-over mechanics that utilized standard Fiat components greatly modified by Ferrari. The flat 8 cylinders availed of 72 hp at 5,500 rpm. Only two models were built: one for Ascari (which was conserved) and one for Marquis Lotario Machiavelli.

32-33 The tail enclosing the 815's rear was typical of the style of the time and the aluminum two-seater could hit 105.4 mph (170 km/h).

TECHNICAL SPECIFICATIONS
AUTO AVIO COSTRUZIONI 815 (1940)

Engine: 8 cylinders in line
91.25 cu. in. (1,496 cc),
bores/stroke: 2.52" x 2.4"
(63 x 60 mm)
Engine weight: 495 lbs. (225 kg)
4 inverted twin carburetors 2.28"/1.44" (32/36 mm)
Power: 72 hp at 6,000 rpm
4-speed gearbox joined to the engine
Tires: Pirelli Stella Bianca 5.50 x 15"
Length: 150" (3,750 mm)
Width: 61.2" (1,530 mm)
Curb-weight: 1,375 lbs. (625 kg)
Speed: from 99.2 to 105.4 mph
(from 160 to 170 km/h)
Consumption: from 3.4 to 3.9 gal/62 mi
(from 13 to 15 l/100 km)

Ferrari 166

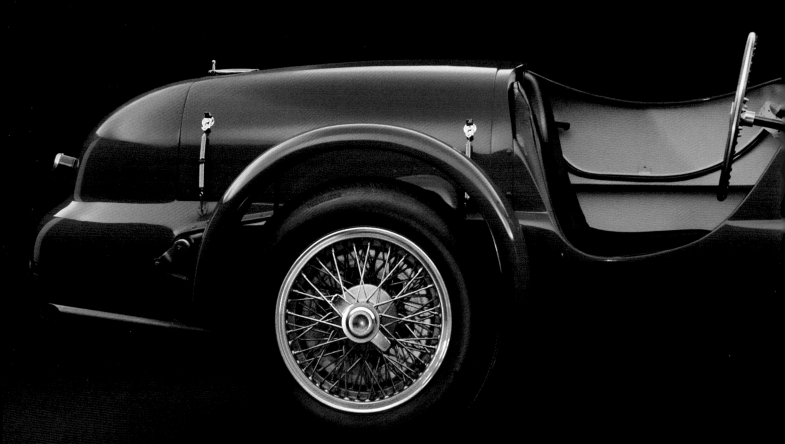

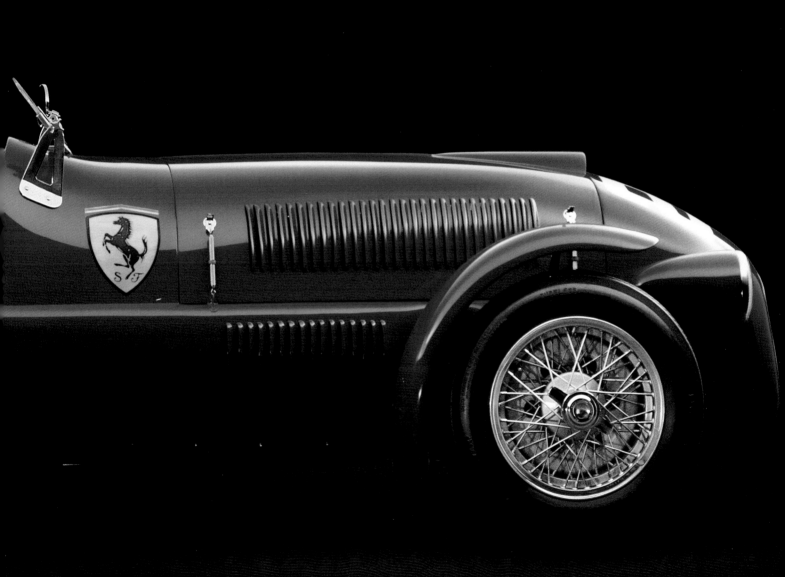

The dream comes true

It was not easy to design an automobile the way Enzo Ferrari desired, but Gioacchino Colombo managed to devise a 12-cylinder that Europe had never seen before. In May 1947, the 125 S started racing, but it was with the 166 that the Ferrari made its real debut in September 1948, at the International Motor Show of Turin. Two different bodies were presented: a coupe, also a 2 +2 seater, at the Touring stand; and, at the Ferrari stand, a sports Spider, renamed "Barchetta" (little boat) because of its particular boat shape – a nickname with which it went down in history. The Barchetta competed in races and won the Tour of Sicily and above all, the Mille Miglia. This was how the "commendatore" himself narrated this event in his memoirs: "This 166 was created as an orthodox car, without any specific experience. We only wanted to build a 12 cylinder of excellence. I have always focused on the importance of engines but not equally so with the chassis, doing my best to achieve great output and performance, certain that this represented more than 50 percent of victories in races." The 12 cylinders were indispensable for Ferrari, but other technicians, such as Busso, also noted this motor's lack of spirit. They said that all would have perhaps preferred a more reliable V8, but in the end, the idea of the 12 cylinders took root, and its initial problems were resolved. In 1949 the victories resumed in the most prestigious testbed ever, the Mille Miglia. These wins were a valid showcase for the 166 Barchetta, which best represented the sports ambitions of the Italians, even though some criticized its reliability and performance. But it made a good impression on Maranello's official driver, Gino Munaron (1928–2009). He knew Luigi Chinetti, who in 1949 had asked him to drive his 166 from Turin up to Le Mans. "I accepted with enthusiasm and it turned out to be an extraordinary experience for me," Munaron recalled. "The 166 was a real fireball of a racecar and just starting up its 12 cylinders was an overwhelming emotion … The V12 and the 140 hp put the drivers to an embarrassing test since they had to keep the car under control with small corrections at the steering wheel even on straight roads because on braking and accelerating, the 166 would start zigzagging and it needed real expertise to tame it. It was a tough and pure automobile with many secrets that only the champions knew; the bends were almost like a survival test the best drivers drove through lightly and stylishly, whereas the others had to undertake tiring corrections with determination. Whether going uphill or downhill, it took the bends with difficulty and you absolutely had to anticipate the trajectories and then, with frequent abrupt turns of the steering wheel, keep it in line, correcting the inevitable back-swerve at the end of the bend where the external wheels, even the rear ones, bore much of the weight, disorienting the driver. The steering was precise but tough and called for real physical and mental effort. The Barchetta I drove to the '24 Hours Le Mans' in 1949 was the same one Chinetti and Lord Selsdon had propelled to the first '24 Hours' victory."

34-35 The Ferrari 166 SC immediately distinguished itself in 1949, both on racetracks and on the road (even Tazio Nuvolari drove this model in 1947 and 1948). It possessed the historical V12 cylinder engine, shown here in the 2-liter version of 130 hp, and was 14.1 ft. (4.3 m) long and had a curb weight of 1,386 lbs. (630 kg). It became the forefather of the future Ferraris.

36-37 The wide right-hand drive compartment could be transformed into a single-seater for track competitions. On the left was a small door and on the right, ample room for the driver's maneuvers.

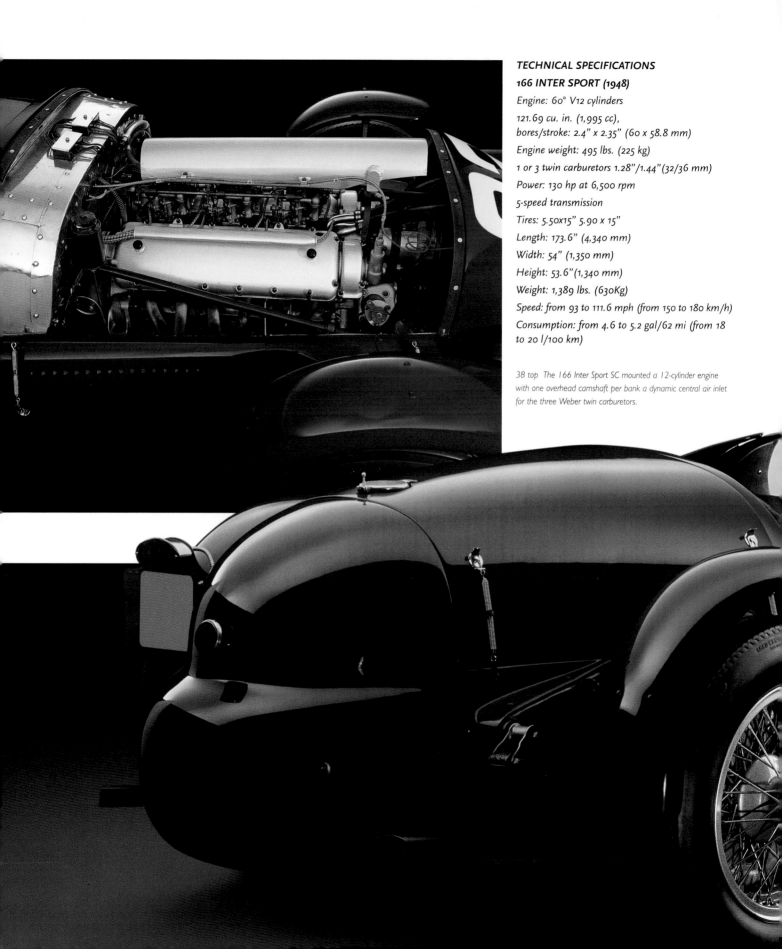

TECHNICAL SPECIFICATIONS
166 INTER SPORT (1948)

Engine: 60° V12 cylinders

*121.69 cu. in. (1,995 cc),
bores/stroke: 2.4" x 2.35" (60 x 58.8 mm)*

Engine weight: 495 lbs. (225 kg)

1 or 3 twin carburetors 1.28"/1.44" (32/36 mm)

Power: 130 hp at 6,500 rpm

5-speed transmission

Tires: 5.50x15" 5.90 x 15"

Length: 173.6" (4,340 mm)

Width: 54" (1,350 mm)

Height: 53.6" (1,340 mm)

Weight: 1,389 lbs. (630Kg)

Speed: from 93 to 111.6 mph (from 150 to 180 km/h)

Consumption: from 4.6 to 5.2 gal/62 mi (from 18 to 20 l/100 km)

38 top The 166 Inter Sport SC mounted a 12-cylinder engine with one overhead camshaft per bank a dynamic central air inlet for the three Weber twin carburetors.

The 166's winning feature? Those who chose it, racers or simply buyers, had no doubt: the extraordinary quality of its engine. Tested for the first time during a race, it then became the protagonist, a feature which all the "true" Ferraris could not forgo. After numerous sports victories (a good 155), the offers of Italian body makers multiplied; the 166 no longer represented an exclusive item of Touring, and even the Farina, Ghia, Bertone and especially Vignale factories offered models that were often impossible to construct in the Maranello facilities.

There was nothing exceptional in the line offered by the Barchetta Tourer, but it conserved a flawless, sober and timeless elegance.

The mechanics, apart from the 12 cylinders, were quite simple, considering the postwar possibilities and the fact that technologies, above all else, targeted the improvement of livability, instead of addressing sports or utilitarian purposes. The first 166 models had a body built of two big longitudinal spars, the main structure on which the reinforcing elements – smaller diameter tubes and transverse pieces – all together formed quite a rigid framework on which the suspensions, brakes and motor were mounted. The orthodox suspensions for 1949 were: quadrilateral and transverse springs in front; at the rear; a rigid bridge with longitudinal springs. The drum brakes were reliable but not always durable. The racecars, however, were all more or less like this. The 128 C engine was an unusual V12 cylinder with an overhead camshaft. It took into account the customer's cravings for power and usage, and was developed over the years to improve output and torque. But the V12 devised by Colombo and overhauled by Lampredi remained a splendid example of Italian handcrafted engineering.

38-39 The fuel tank with a capacity of 19.5 gal. (75 liters) and the 15-inch spare tire were set at the wide tail.

TECHNICAL SPECIFICATIONS

340-342 AMERICA (1951–1953)

Engine: 60° V12 cylinders

156.34 cu. in. (2,563 cc),
bores/stroke: 3.2" x 2.72" (80 x 68 mm)

3 twin carburetors 40 DCF

Power: 200 hp at 5,000 rpm

4-speed transmission

Tires: 640 x 15"

Length: 164" (4,100 mm)

Width: 60" (1,500 mm)

Height: 55.2" (1,380 mm)

Weight: 2,640 lbs. (1,200 kg)

Speed: 148.8 mph (240 km/h)

Out to conquer America

How could Enzo Ferrari resist the United States' alluring requests for quality sports cars like those of Maranello? Its artisanal production, limited to about 10 units per year, thus extremely flexible, was able to meet the various market demands. Furthermore, the skillful driver-manager, Luigi Chinetti, was there to keep the rich American reservoir alive. He was always ready to welcome the Ferrari race-cars in a sector occupied by the English with their old, stylish cars, whereas the Germans were still concentrated in rebuilding their factories. The real "made in the U.S.A." sports cars were practically nonexistent. With such a renowned name in the race circuits, it was really not difficult to sell to the very rich Americans (though not many) Maranello's gems that had even starred in famous films.

The United States met the Prancing Horse's new car series with enthusiasm, and brought new revenues to Maranello's insatiable coffers. The first among the 340 America specials were presented at the International Motor Show of Turin in March 1951, and sported a new 4101.66cc/250 cu. in. (4.1 liter) engine derived directly from the so-called "Lampredi" family, suitable for cars with big engine displacements and destined to reap great success in sports competitions in the years to follow. The Italian body makers concentrated their efforts on this propulsion unit, fascinated by the exclusive and powerful 12 cylinders. The first 340 America, a name that announced the unitary engine displacement – 20.74 cu. in. (340 cc), precisely, for a total of 4,102 – dressed by Touring, was still in vogue at Maranello and boasted of a power from 220 hp to 6,000 revolutions, initially unthinkable especially for racing competitions, immediately became a sporty roadster. As for the other Ferrari cars, the Ghia also offered a 340 America two-seater plus two (reproduced in other prototypes) and entered Argentine President Juan Perón's Ferrari collection. However, Vignal produced particularly the more sportive cars, whereas Pininfarina did not present any of his elegant items but dedicated himself to the succeeding series.

From 1951 to 1953, there were 22 340 America cars out of a total of 77, and they immediately demonstrated their strength by winning the Mille Miglia 1951 with Luigi Villoresi, and then the Portugal Grand Prix. Competitive qualities, together with the unmistakable Italian elegance of the bodyworks, determined this car's success, further pursued in the succeeding 342 series (six units produced), which repeated its mechanical characteristics but changed its name and diminished the output by 20 hp, to make it easier and more enjoyable to drive. Even the new series had the same finishing features of the Ferrari in those years: leather interior, as desired by the buyers of such expensive cars, and a livable aspect that paid scarce attention to the passengers until the clients overseas started demanding more ample room. The front seats were quite comfy, whereas the backseats called for a bit of sacrifice (on the other hand, the Ferrari customer had well defined characteristics). The dashboard, almost always metallic and without finishing, was dominated by two big devices (speedometer and rev counter), and an array of other levers triggered the various (and few) services available then. The right-hand driver's seat evidenced its clear-cut racing origin with an almost horizontal steering column and wooden Nardi steering wheel that enhanced the outstretched position of the arms. Of course the various controls were mechanical: in those times power steering was still unheard of. The passengers seated in the back could enjoy the deep and overwhelming roar of the 12 cylinders, but it was certainly not very comfortable. On the other hand the Ferrari users did not demand this type of quality, but rather expressed strong emotions, and Ferrari knew how to satisfy them. There were not many clients for the succeeding 342 model: of more than 44 Ferrari cars sold from September 1951 to the start of 1953, only six were 342 America models. However, one was bought by King Leopold III of Belgium.

42-43 The 342 had classic, impeccable Pininfarina lines that enchanted even Leopold III of Belgium, though not all liked the dual air inlets on the hood. Only six 342 models were made during a three-year production of 44 cars.

44 top The 342 Vignale at the Mille Miglia race in 1952: it behaved well throughout the season but was discontinued after Rome.

44-45 The 342 Pininfarina was built also in the Berlinetta version, which adopted the sportier right-hand drive.

45

Ferrari 212 Export

The V12 makes progress

When the first 212 appeared for the first time in April 1951, the name Ferrari was still unknown in motoring circles. Race drivers, important managers, outstanding celebrities and actors often appeared in newsmagazines with their Ferraris and more than ever, owning a Ferrari became an extraordinary status symbol. Italy had only around 465,000 cars circulating: it took 12 months of work to buy a utility car, whereas the quality of welfare services, healthcare and education was scarce. The Italian industry, however, had awakened: Fiat's 500 B dominated the market, and the company also offered the very American 1400. Then two newly built gems, the Alfa Romeo 1900 and the Lancia Aurelia, took command among the up-market cars. Italy's chassis designers, however, had an insight: the fact that the cars bearing the Prancing Horse symbol (only 33 in 1951) were the rarest and most precious and would ensure great profits. Ghia even built an American-type coupe for the Argentinean president, Juan Péron. Touring proceeded with the style of the 166, and Pininfarina (the name is still the same today) started his partnership with Maranello, which has continued up to the present. They built 15 coupes and cabriolets ordered by outstanding celebrities, such as the Princess of Belgium and Liliana of Rethy, a steady client of the Prancing Horse. Subsequently, Touring, the most traditional of all, presented coupe and barchetta models along the line of the preceding 166, like that of race driver Mike Hawthorn. Vignale was the one who produced the greatest number of beautiful sports 212, as well as high-powered cars. All manufacturers by then had adopted some of the classical Ferrari style lines, such as the grilles with rectangular elements and the wire-spoke wheels. Some, like Marzotto, even wanted to innovate: just imagine the 212 race model with a Fountain body nicknamed "Egg" because of its bizarre shape.

The manufacturing process for these Ferrari models was outstanding and exclusive: the bodies, practically hand-wrought, were sent to Maranello where the machines were mounted, then tested on Via Emilia and the surrounding district, and finally subjected to approval by the "commendatore." Precisely in 1951–1953, 47 Inter cars were produced in Maranello, which summed up to 80 units of the Export models (according to off-record sources), reaffirming the interest of the wealthier markets. The 212, in the unceasing evolutionary atmosphere of Maranello, lasted only two years, and in 1952, a much more competitive and reliable car, the renowned 250 GT, was produced.

TECHNICAL SPECIFICATIONS
212 EXPORT AND INTER (1951)
Engine: 60° V12 cylinders
156.34 cu. in. (2,563 cc.),
bores/stroke: 2.4" x 2.35" (68 x 58.8 mm)
1 or 3 twin-carburetors 1.44" (36 mm)
Power: 165 hp at 7,000 rpm
5-speed transmission
Tires: 5.90 x 16"
Length: 164" (4,100 mm)
Width: 60" (1,500 mm)
Height: 55.2" (1,380 mm)
Weight: 1,854 lbs. (850 kg)
Speed: 137 mph
(220 km/h)

Its features

Though there were not many opportunities in those times to do great tests on the new models, to avoid all risks, everyone started off from tested mechanics, and even the 212 contained solutions traceable to the previous Ferrari with V12 motors designed by Gioacchino Colombo, upgraded to the desired 156.34 cu. in. (2,563 cc) with 150-170 hp, and one or more twin-choke carburetors. We are speaking of exclusive sports models that ensured high performance but not very comfortable travel. The framework, in turn, conserved schemes that Ferrari held dear, such as the massive spars and metallic crosspieces with quadrilateral oscillating suspensions on the front and rigid bridge at the rear with upper struts and springs. This conservative (but efficient) scheme was completed by a 5-speed gearbox, drum brakes, worm-and-roller steering and hydraulic shock absorbers. For years Ferrari would have maintained these schemes tested in races for the "pure" sports cars. The 212 played its role in boosting Maranello's competitive spirit, winning minor races such as the Tour of Sicily in 1951 with Vittorio Marzotton making third place during the Mille Miglia that same year. These cars were difficult to handle due to their exuberating power especially on bends; the foreign testers were enthusiastic about the engine, but not about the stiff and imprecise gears. The Italian drivers were satisfied with the powerful and elastic 12 cylinders, but very cautious in assessing the 212, which often tended to swerve crosswise on bends, a fault difficult to correct; furthermore, the brakes easily lost their effectiveness when overly engaged.

50 and 50-51 The 212's engine with 12 cylinders and 3 Weber 36 DCF twin carburetors.
On the left the 212 Export by Vignale, a one-off model in blue-green, now belongs to an American collector. Umberto Marzotto drove it in the sixth Dolomite Cup and also won the 1951 Trieste-Opicina race.

52-53 *This brassy 212 by Vignale was evidently rebodied. It may have been an Inter or Export version: 86 units were built, in the sedan or Spider versions.*

The 1950s:

The Roaring Years

AT THE START OF THE 1950S, ITALY'S AUTOMOTIVE INDUSTRY WAS STILL POOR AND PRODUCED FEWER THAN 80,000 CARS, MOSTLY FIAT 500 C – THE CHEAPEST CAR ON THE MARKET (625,000 LIRE) – WHILE THE OTHER TWO HOUSES, LANCIA AND ALFA, BUILT A LIMITED NUMBER. WORD OF THE FERRARIS HAD ALREADY GOTTEN AROUND, ESPECIALLY IN SPORTS CIRCLES, AND SINCE MARANELLO'S PRODUCTION AT THE TIME WAS VERY INCONSISTENT, IT CONCENTRATED MAINLY ON SPORTS CARS. BEING SUCH A SKILLFUL ADMINISTRATOR, FERRARI HAD ALREADY FORESEEN THAT TO BUILD HIS REPUTATION, VICTORIES ON THE TRACK OR IN THE MILLE MIGLIA WERE CRUCIAL. IN THE MEANTIME, HE BUILT HIS PRESTIGIOUS AND INCOMPARABLE (AT LEAST WITH RESPECT TO THE ITALIAN PRODUCTIONS) SPORTS CARS. FERRARI'S PRODUCTION WAS PRACTICALLY AT A HAND-CRAFTED LEVEL: IT HAD 300 EMPLOYEES AND IN 1956 PRODUCED 81 CARS. THIS NUMBER MAY HAVE SEEMED DISCOURAGING BUT IT WAS CERTAINLY NOT SO FOR ENZO FERRARI, WHO IN 1950 EVEN RESOLVED TO BEAT THE LEADER OF THE GRAND PRIX, THAT IS, THE 158-159 OF ALFA ROMEO DESIGNED RIGHT IN HIS FACTORY IN 1938. HE WOULD SUCCEED IN THIS STRENUOUS CHASE IN 1951, WHEN ALBERTO ASCARI IN A FERRARI BATTLED WITH JUAN MANUEL FANGIO TO THE VERY END OF THE GRAND PRIX TO WIN THE WORLD TITLE. THE VICTORY WAS FUNDAMENTAL TO THE "COMMENDATORE," BUT IN REALITY HE HAD ALREADY ACHIEVED IT: HIS NAME AND CARS HAD BECOME FAMOUS THE WORLD OVER, EVEN ON THE VERY RICH U.S. MARKET, WHERE HIS TRUSTED AGENT, LUIGI CHINETTI, WORKED WITH GREAT PROFICIENCY. OF COURSE, THE INITIAL PRODUCTION WAS NOT REMARKABLE BUT THE PRANCING HORSE'S SINGLE-SEATERS HAD ALREADY WON FOUR FORMULA ONE WORLD TITLES, EIGHT MILLE MIGLIA TITLES, TWO CARRERA PANAMERICANA TITLES AND HUNDREDS OF VERY IMPORTANT RACES. DURING THE DECADE IN QUESTION, PRODUCTION HAD ALMOST DOUBLED (248 CARS WITH 350 EMPLOYEES). MARANELLO HAD BECOME BY THEN A CONSOLIDATED EMPIRE.

Ferrari 375 America

56-57 The most classic among the 375 Americas of 1953 bore the Pininfarina signature. This model looked like a sedate coupe but in reality its V12 274.59 cu. in. (4.5-liter) engine delivered a good 300 hp and hit a top speed of 155 mph (250 km/h). Weighing 2,530 lbs. (1,150 kg), the sports car 375 MM version, lightened and with a reduced wheelbase, could reach 340 hp and won many races.

58 King Leopold III of Belgium, a faithful Maranello client, is shown here with the 375 MM of 1974 together with Battista "Pinin" Farina. The car mounted the more powerful 375 Plus engine (330 hp at 6,000 rpm).

Dollars and horsepower

Enzo Ferrari felt increasingly attracted to the enticement of the United States, and Luigi Chinetti, his right-hand man there, had the necessary backing to "place" the Prancing Horse's automobiles on the market.

The 375 America entered this sphere of interest for that market and also gained the upper hand in the design of new mechanics. There already was a concrete base for that 12-cylinder engine that had given the Alfa Romeo such a hard time during the first Formula One world championships. Such a versatile and multifunctional engine managed to adapt itself to all the requests, even those from America. Apart from the engines, this 375 was interesting since it was identical to the 250 Europa, which had "smaller" 12 cylinders, that is, of 183.06 cu. in. (3 liters). As to the finishing of the chassis for America, the "commendatore" addressed Pininfarina, the man who knew how to interpret Ferrari's tastes and especially that of the Ferrari faithful, who generally preferred moderation even in the stylistic solutions. This splendid 375 of 1953, a two-seater plus two, was devised to satisfy the most demanding sportsmen of those times. If Pininfarina was the person who best interpreted Ferrari mechanics, Alfredo Vignale, another giant of that age and already an author of other previous Ferrari models,

dedicated himself to the "America" with a charming U.S.-styled Spider. The aspect of this 375, despite Pininfarina's skillful touches, felt the effects of its dimensions and the longest wheelbase of all the Ferrari productions, 112 in. (2,800 mm). This stately coupe was characterized by a small roof panel generally of a different color from the rest of the body, underscoring the car's dimensions even more, and is still very impressive today, with a great, immense hood. Pininfarina, however, indulged himself on this bodywork, and produced splendid custom-built cars that distinguished themselves in the main Motor Shows of those years, always with the prerogative of evidencing the great hood like the one-off versions ordered for Ingrid Bergman and Giovanni Agnelli, which showed the stylistic solutions repeated on the Ferrari (Testarossa, Dino 206, 328 GTB, Mondial model) and also on those of other sports car manufacturers. An unforgettable Spider 375 Plus was prepared in 1955 for King Leopold III of Belgium, not to mention the racecar models, such as the 375 MM. The 375 America lasted for two years, up to the end of 1955, when it was replaced by a similar model, the 410, also designed for the United States. The number of 375 models manufactured during those two years is uncertain – probably about 10.

58-59 Aggressive and enticing, the 375 MM was designed to compete in races. Lightened to 1,980 lbs. (900 kg) compared to the 375 America (2,535 lbs.; 1,150 kg), it also had a wheelbase shortened from 112 in. (2,800 mm) to 104 in. (2,600 mm). Mighty and slender, the 375 MM Berlinetta by Pininfarina took command in several races, and in 1954 underwent a transformation, becoming the 375 Plus Barchetta (first with 347 hp and later even 370 hp) that won the most important events of the year, the World Championships for the Sport category, the 24 Hours of Le Mans and La Carrera Panamericana.

TECHNICAL SPECIFICATIONS

375 AMERICA (1952–1953)

Engine: 60° V12 cylinders

275.84 cu. in. (4,522 cc),
bores/stroke: 3.36" x 2.72" (84 x 68 mm)

3 twin carburetors 40 DCF

Power: 300 hp at 6,300 rpm

4-speed transmission

Tires: 7.10 x 15"

Wheelbase: 112" (2,800 mm)

Curb-weight: 2,530 lbs. (1,150 kg)

Speed: 155 mph (250 km/h)

Conservative mechanics

Already in 1953, Maranello could avail itself of all the material it needed to affirm the prestige Ferrari so desired. So for this 375 model, the concepts used for previous experiments were used again. The motor with "Lampredi" initials gave the best guarantees for both normal and racing uses – as would be demonstrated on the mightier 375 Plus version, equipped with a more efficient De Dion bridge in place of the longitudinal springs. But above all, it was with the powerful 340 hp engine (and also the 370 hp) that the 375 Plus managed to assert itself in important races such as the 24 Hours Spa (1953) and the 1,000 km (621 mi.) in Buenos Aires (1954). The mechanics expressed the same concepts as the prior models: a chassis with huge spars inspired by those of the other Maranello sports cars of those times. The suspensions were typical of the Ferrari cars then, with semielliptic springs and the Houdaille hydraulic shock absorbers, all weighing heavily, and therefore demonstrating conservative mechanics that would appear for years in the Ferraris. On the V12 motor, as already underlined, was the "long" unit bearing the "Lampredi" mark, for the huge models, with an overhead camshaft and three vertical quadrilateral carburetors for a significant output (300 hp), mounted (and upgraded to 370 hp) on the racecar models such as the 375 MM.

60 and 60-61 The 375 America's chassis displayed Pininfarina at his best. This anomalous coupe (for Gianni Agnelli) with vertical grille, panoramic windshield and tailfins, displayed the style lines that would show up also on the following Ferraris.

64-65 and 66-67 A 375 MM, this is an elegant Berlinetta Pininfarina of 1955 equipped with slightly accentuated rear tail fins. A remarkable output of 340 hp at 6,500 rpm according to ratios; its speed could reach up to 167.4 mph (270 km/h).

Ferrari 250 GT California

The prettiest, the most desired

One of a kind, it immediately became a collector's car, as Enzo Ferrari desired. Once again, he did not ignore the suggestions of Luigi Chinetti, who knew exactly where to "place" the cars that bore the indelible Prancing Horse badge, being a profound expert of the tastes and possibilities of the Americans. And yet the Spiders and the Cabriolets were not too appreciated in Italy where the coupe was preferred, even if in those times the "open" models were produced and became popular worldwide, like the Giulietta Spider or the Aurelia B24. The California was not the first Ferrari Spider endowed with a strong personality: there were already those branded Pininfarina, Vignale, Touring and Boano. But none were loved as much as the California, judged as the prettiest and certainly the most exciting: a true and proper, unequalled example of design, to be driven and conserved with love. On the other hand, its name clearly indicated its destiny: the roads of California, with its warm climate and the rich drivers, truly special automobile enthusiasts. And this Spider was exceptional: born as Ferrari wished, as a racecar (no wonder it was built at Scaglietti's), thanks to its thrilling drive and aggressive lines. Essential but so enthralling, it achieved immediate success.

The first prototypes Maranello produced in December 1957 were almost all destined for the United States. The car was stylistically perfect; however, it was continually overhauled mechanically and stylistically with a carryover of data obtained (a typical Ferrari custom) from the races, given that those were the sensations the California was supposed to transmit. The reference point was obviously the unbeatable 250 GT Berlinetta, and so in 1959 more efficient Dunlop disc brakes were added in place of the drum versions. In 1960 the shorter wheelbase and chassis appeared, from 8.52 to 7.87 ft. (2.60 to 2.40 m), and remained in production up to the last 1963 model. There were 55 of these "short wheelbase" versions, against the 51 "long wheelbase" models, but the figures in all the Ferrari productions of those years are uncertain. In all the models, however, the balance of the bodywork remained flawless whether in aluminum or steel. All 106 units built by Scaglietti from 1957 to 1962 are very rare samples for car collectors. The lines of the California were faultless, with an almost perfect balance between the various volumes; the flank slowly descended to meet the tough and prominent rear fenders that gave impetus to the whole car, harmonized by skillful touches which only "good old" Pininfarina knew how to achieve. These included some "racing" features like faired lights and the convertible top, air scoops on the hood and air vents on the sides. All were well supported on big wheels with 16-inch spokes. The California once again took up the 250 GT SWB technologies and made use of the experience acquired in the Berlinetta races. However, given its structure, weighing about 220 lbs. (100 kg) more, it could rarely compete with the "closed" models. It was also overhauled during its lifespan, with modifications: for example, after the first 15 models, the fairing of the lights was eliminated, and in 1959 disc brakes were added. As Enzo Ferrari envisioned, the California had to convey all the emotions of a racecar equipped for daily use. And the undertaking succeeded because the car relayed unforgettable sensations while achieving honorable performance. Prices were sky-high for those times: 5 million lire against half a million for a Fiat 500. Among the distinguished owners were film director Roger Vadim with Brigitte Bardot; actor James Coburn; writer Françoise Sagan; tenor Mario Del Monacotenor; Count Volpi di Misurata; and Ferrari driver Wolfgang von Trips.

68-69 The 250 GT California of 1957 designed by Pininfarina, built in steel or aluminum by Scaglietti, combines incomparable elegance with sporty aggressiveness (240-280 hp). It was discontinued in 1963 but the 106 units produced were flawless.

70-71 The California's style lines had not changed despite the variable wheelbase. A total of 106 units were built by Scaglietti (55 with short wheelbase, 51 with long wheelbase).

72-73 The hard top was not very suitable but the impetus of this splendid chassis had not changed. Disc brakes were mounted from 1959 onward.

TECHNICAL SPECIFICATIONS
250 GT CALIFORNIA (1957–1963)
Engine: 60° V12 cylinders
180.13 cu. in. (2,953 cc),
bores/stroke: 2.94" x 2.35" (73.5 x 58.8 mm)
3 twin carburetors 40 DCL
Power: from 240 to 280 hp at 7,500 rpm
4-speed synchronized transmission
Tires: 6.00 x 16"
Wheelbase: from 104" to 96"
(from 2,600 to 2,400 mm)
Curb-weight: 2,420 lbs. (1,100 kg)
2,200 lbs. (1,000 kg) (SWB)
Speed: 166.16 mph (268 km/h)
Length: 166" (4,150 mm)
Width: 67.6" (1,690 mm)
Height: 50.4"
(1,260 mm)

74-75 *The carburetor air inlets on the hood were the distinguishing marks of the California. The built-in ones distinguished the short wheelbase (SWB) model of 1960.*

76-77 *The very powerful 12-cylinder engine of 183.06 cu. in. (3 liters) was the California's strong point and was the main protagonist of high performance: it could push up to 161.55 mph (260 km/h).*

The 1960s:

Decisive Years also for Cars

THE AUTOMOBILE HAD DECISIVELY AND ALMOST BOLDLY BROKEN INTO THE HOMES OF ITALIANS, WHO NOW COULD AFFORD ALL TYPES OF CARS, STARTING WITH THE TINY UTILITY CARS OF FIAT (THE 500 SURPASSED 2 MILLION UNITS REGISTERED AND COST 567,000 LIRE), FOLLOWED BY THE OTHER FIATS IN A MARKET THAT PASSED THE 1.2 MILLION MARK BY THE END OF THE DECADE. THE FIRST FOREIGNER WAS THE SIMCA (ALSO PARTLY ITALIAN), WHICH PLACED 10TH WITH 160,000 UNITS, FOLLOWED CLOSELY BY THE REVOLUTIONARY ENGLISH MINI BUILT IN ITALY. BUT NOW THE ITALIANS COULD INDULGE THEMSELVES IN THE "FORBIDDEN FRUIT" OF FOREIGN CARS. FERRARI HAD A HIGHLY PRESTIGIOUS PRODUCTION, AND OVER A 10-YEAR PERIOD SURPASSED 7,000 UNITS; ITS CARS COST AT LEAST 6.5 MILLION LIRE, BUT THE LIST INCLUDED THE PRESTIGIOUS DAYTONA AND THE LITTLE DINO 206, THE FIRST OF FERRARI'S "ALL-REAR" SERIES. IN SPORTS F1, TWO WORLD TITLES (DRIVERS AND CONSTRUCTORS) WERE ACHIEVED, ALL WITH REAR ENGINES, BESIDES THE NUMEROUS WINS AND TITLES IN THE SPORT PROTOTIPO AND GRAN TURISMO CATEGORIES. THERE WAS AN ATMOSPHERE OF CONCRETE HOPE FOR THE DECADE TO COME.

Ferrari 250 GT SWB

Descriptions of the 250 GT could fill an entire library since so many books, articles, essays and legends have always revolved around this Ferrari model with its power output, sports triumphs and the numerous heirs that have completed its dynasty. The car was the fruit of the Maranello technicians' continuous research, tests and races. It was a V12 engine, created in 1947 as a 91.5 cu. in. (1500 cc) which in a few years increased to 183 cu. in. (3000 cc), winning races such as the Mille Miglia, 24 Hours of Le Mans and the Mexican Carrera, and also paraded in triumph through the streets of the entire world. In 1951, the Ferrari production of just 33 cars was certainly not great, but Maranello wanted to grow and so when it found the ideal 12-cylinder engine, it immediately tested it in the race par excellence, the Mille Miglia. The 183.06 cu. in. (3-liter) engine displacement for the 250 GT was the ideal one for both racing and production models. The first test came about in the historical Mille Miglia of 1952, when Bracco's 250 S beat the big Mercedes team. After this victory, Ferrari widened its objectives and targeted the new 183.06 cu. in. (3 liters). At the Paris Motor Show in 1954, the "commendatore" with his supercar was a protagonist. He presented the 375 America and 250 GT Europa and paved the way for a long series of derivative models that reaped success. With these Grand Tourers Pininfarina and Ferrari best expressed their mastery in the more sporty or custom-built models for special clients. The shape of the 250 GT found greater equilibrium, thanks to their more compact dimensions and the new "short" wheelbase engines. All exuded the same "family feeling" of a particular design, high sides, reduced wheelbase and passenger compartments, streamlined features that gave an exclusive

80-81 Another of Maranello's legendary cars, built in 1959 but distributed throughout the 1960s. The SWB was considered the ideal sports car; 162 units were sold, dominating the races and gaining renown thanks to its fantastic Pininfarina line built by Scaglietti.

82-83 This splendid custom-built Pininfarina was built on a 250 GT chassis, with features that set the trend for future models. It was a unique 1955 model for John Murray, and was unusually beautiful with rear "tail fins."

personality to the Ferrari cars. The 250 GTs manufactured in that period made use of small, continuous improvements, tested in races and in the production of each model. The design was always
signed by Pininfarina, but the building of the body
shell was entrusted also to other suppliers like Ellena, Boano or Scaglietti, who worked directly with
Maranello. The mechanics were developed almost
day by day: the 250 GT won all the Grand Touring
races, like the so-called "Tour de France" of 1958,
displaying champions like Willy Mairesse, Olivier
Gendebien and Jean Guichet.

TECHNICAL SPECIFICATIONS
250 GT A SHORT WHEELBASE (SWB) (1961)
Engine: 60° V12 cylinders
180.13 cu. in. (2953 cc),
bores/stroke: 2.94" x 2.35" (73.5 x 58.8 mm)
3 twin carburetors 40 DCN
Power: from 240 to 280 hp at 7,500 rpm
synchronized 4-speed transmission
Tires: 185 x 16" 6.00 x 16" (racing)
Curb-weight: 2,112 lbs. (960 kg)
Speed: 166 mph (268 km/h)
Length: 166" (4,150 mm)
Width: 67.4" (1,690 mm)
Height: 50.4" (1,260 mm)

The most famous among the 259 Berlinettas made their debut in 1961. The most expert Ferrari fans are well aware that this 250 GT was nicknamed SWB, meaning "short wheelbase" – 96 in. (2400 mm), 8 in. (200 mm) less – because the reduced distance between the front and rear axle enhanced its easy drive and performance compared to the other 250 models. The "short wheelbase" was considered the ideal sports car for its behavior on the road and on the track, where it was almost unbeatable. Still designed by Pininfarina and built by Scaglietti, its aggressive lines are still fascinating today. It debuted in 1959 when the Italian industry produced 390,000 cars, almost all Fiat 600s or 500s (Ferrari produced just 241). Only seven "interim" versions (long-wheelbase, 2.6 ft. or 260 m) were produced in 1959, preceding the birth of the "short wheelbase" by a few months. The car was an immediate success with the Ferrari clientele and was offered in two versions, a racer type in aluminum and another roadster version in steel, both built by Scaglietti. Its lines synthesized the rapid evolution of the Maranello sports cars, which benefitted from the Pininfarina touch, the Scaglietti construction and a good aerodynamic coefficient (Cx = 0.33). The SWBs produced as of 1962 totaled 162: 90 roadsters and 72 race models. The 250 GT's technical supremacy was also due to the new engine with split power ducts to favor the flow of gas and improve output, which even reached 280 hp. Though the chassis and the suspensions followed tradition, they benefitted from the continuous lessons learned from the races and became stiffer, perfecting the drive. Disc brakes were also adopted, giving another advantage to the 250 SWB. The gear became only a 4-speed progressive transmission, thanks to the greater exploitation of the engine. The project was supervised by the engineers, Chiti, Bizzarrini and Forghieri, who worked together also for the future GTOs. The fame of the "short wheelbase" did not decline in time, but intensified due to all the victories achieved, because of the emotions the V12 aroused and also for its fascinating lines. The list of winners of the most important races highlights the most outstanding names of the world's racing elite: Stirling Moss, Mike Parkes, Willy Mairesse and the Rodriguez brothers, and Graham Hill. Those who had the good fortune to drive it still remember with pleasure its debut at Le Mans in 1959. It was much easier to drive than its ancestors, thanks to the better exploitability of the V12, which in progression could also shoot up to 7500 rpm; the 4-speed (but also 5) transmission well exploited the engine's characteristics and allowed it to take the curves faster, thanks to the grip guaranteed by the chassis. Stirling Moss affirmed: "That V12 seemed to have 300 hp, around twenty more than what was declared."

The passion for this 250 GT was infinite. Among the numberless books on this theme, one in particular stands out, written by an English author and owner of a 250 GT, wherein the vicissitudes of all the models are described, as well as the list of owners in whose hands the cars transited. Not a very easy job, given the difficulty in gathering all the data, but this underscores the infinite passion the true Ferrari enthusiasts nurture for these cars which are really one of a kind.

86-87 One of the many 250 GTs produced by Maranello. They were called the SWBs short wheelbase from 8.52 ft. (2.60 m) to 7.87 ft. (2.40 m). It set a production record for those times (over 100 units). It made a name for itself, thanks to its sports victories worldwide, from Europe to America. Built in steel or aluminum, this beautiful SWB is one of the most stunning GTs ever, and is very much sought after in auctions of the sector.

Ferrari 250 GTO

With racing in your blood

88-89 A shot of the most classic versions of the 1962 GTO. Conceived by Ferrari engineer Giotto Bizzarrini, it was built by Scaglietti with the typical cooling slits on the sides.

90-91 The 1964 GTO bore the same mechanics as the first GTO of 300 hp. The nose was wider by 8.5 cm (1.755 m), longer by 10 cm (4.45 m) and shorter by 9.5 cm (1.152 m).

Destiny can be strange ... even for cars. Take the GTO for example: the Grand Touring Homologated series was created at a particular moment of Enzo Ferrari's life when his creations had to battle against the forces of new figures in England and Germany. In 1962, when Italy registered 491,000 cars, of which only 33,000 were foreign makes, the Marche World Championship, reserved for the Grand Tourers, was held and Maranello's throne seemed to waver. Furthermore, just at that moment almost the entire staff assigned to the project abandoned the Mother House. However, in 1961 Ferrari had already planned for the following year's world championship

and in anticipation had given a preview of his preparations. So at the Monza Grand Prix in 1961, the Berlinetta prototype, differing from the previous models, was entrusted the task of conquering that world title, which Ferrari greatly desired. The "GTO" officially debuted at the product launch in February 1962, where its new shape surprised everyone. It appeared with a chassis that was still traditional, in tubes and spars, in an attempt to make the theories of the aerodynamics prophet, Prof. Wunibald Kamm, coexist with Ferrari's racing traditions. So creation of was created one of the strangest but best-loved Ferrari cars, also one of the most appreciated in auc-

tions. The minimum indispensable of 36 cars were made, to which seven units of the second model were added in 1964.

This exceptional car pursued the Maranello tradition, but it also offered innovative and original solutions, especially in aerodynamics – no longer provided by Pininfarina, but by young engineers: firstly, Giotto Bizzarrini, and later, Mauro Forghieri. At the start it did not seem so attractive (it was nicknamed "duckling") but subsequently, thanks to all the victories and to its harsh efficiency, it conquered everyone. Bizzarrini created a body that would wrap around the mechanics, in view of the problems of the earlier SWB, especially at high speeds. So it had a nose that was as low as it could go, a curvaceous shape, a small grille, and a chipped tail with the small transversal *spoiler* to better direct the air flow and create less turbulence. To improve the cooling of the engine shaft, three louvers (closable) were practically applied at the hood's base. Other air vents on the sides speeded up the circulation of air. These aerodynamic solutions obtained the desired effects, giv-

en the victories in the road races (Targa Florio or Tour de France) and on racetracks (24 Hours of Le Mans, Nurbürgring, Monza) and the three consecutive World Championships (from 1962 to 1964). The mechanics – such as the V12 of 300 hp inherited from the Prototype 250 P, with dry sump lubrication, 5-speed gearbox and disc brakes – benefitted from the races.

New solutions were continually experimented on, also for the chassis: besides the spars, an ulterior reinforcing trellis framework of small-diameter tubes made the structure more rigid and thus more precise at the wheel. At the rear were the rigid bridge with springs and the addition of coil springs on the telescopic dampers. Other details, such as the transversal rods and trailing arms, made the rear axle reaction and also the drive even easier to handle. The entire project was in progress because the young technicians were continuously searching for new solutions, contradicting the widespread opinion that Ferrari technology was immobile, as compared to the progress made in races.

The GTO's compartment evidenced only the pursuit of minimum weight, without attention to comfort or refurbishing: a racecar with seats perfunctorily upholstered, a turret for "worm and sector" steering and nothing more (it did not even have an odometer), and winding Plexiglas windows. Some clients tried to refine it through the setup. The engine was that of the Testarossa (with dry sump), thus it was a pure racecar that maintained the efficiency of its predecessors. In 1966 after more than 200 wins, the GTO concluded its brilliant career. Fifty years have passed since its debut and today, it requires long heating-up operations before it can give its best. Within the first meters it needs time to tune into the driver's wavelength, after which, as the drivers and owners have always declared, its drive becomes an explosion of incredible sensations, even on normal roads. No other can ever compare with this car, and it is still driven today, but of course, with due precautions, as befit a 50-year-old.

91 *The GTO's V12 remained the 183.06-cu. in. (3-liter) version with 300 hp but some also mounted a 244.08-cu. in. (4-liter) engine.*

Ferrari 275 GTB

Back to sports

News and rumors fly fast in Romagna, and certainly the manufacturers of that golden automobile sector, the people who built the most popular Grand Tourers of those times, were aware of their competitors' projects. So the three automakers, Ferrari, Maserati and Lamborghini, prepared ambitious battle plans, with small masterpieces, such as the 275 GTB-GTB/4. The car was built in 1964; while the Prancing Horse finally regained the Formula One World Championship from the English, the Sport models restated their supremacy over Ford and Porsche, and the GTO was always the strongest among the GTs. The new 275 GTB was a 201.3 cu. in. (3,300 cc) model that left everyone breathless: with 280 hp and an all-curvy figure by Pininfarina, only a two-seater, with a long hood that evidenced its output and a clipped tail (still in Kamm style), and a *spoiler* exalting its sportive features. It was 173 in. (4,325 mm) long, like an average-displacement engine, and beyond its figure, possessed a lot of peculiarities, such as the transmission moved to the rear drive train, the new suspensions with independent wheels, and rims in alloy. This was undoubtedly an in- novative Ferrari, which a year later would already have a new, more streamlined muzzle, more stable at top speeds. In 1965, Ferrari produced more than 740 of the 250 GTBs; this increased by a hundred in 1966, when the car was replaced by the more refined GTB/4, which was even more brassy. Even the interior reflected the model's sporting mark in all its components, starting with the driver's position, rather sunken, with arms fully stretched, enough space for two, and traditional Italian-style installations, that took into account the demands of the 1960s and the GTB philosophy. All the instruments,

speedometer and rev counter stood out, with six other, much smaller ones on the dashboard together with the commands for the various services. All the rest was also sportive, the Nardo steering wheel in wood and 5-speed gearbox with typical racing sector engagement. There were no electrical commands, air-conditioning or radio. The boot was small, just enough to host two small suitcases and the spare tire. The rear bench served only for the baggage.

Its 12-cylinder engine was the natural evolution of the 1947 model, heightened to the utmost develop-ment thanks to six twin-choke carburetors and continuous overhauls. The rest also changed: the rear-axle transmission with independent wheels was a real novelty in Ferrari production. The other revolution was seen a year later, when in the GTB/4 series, always aiming to oppose the growing competition, it adopted the overhead four-cam engine with 300 hp and the new 5-speed transmission (Porsche synchronized) on the rear axle and clutch assembled as a unit with the engine. The driveshaft was now housed in a rigid tube, which not only improved drivability, but also silenced the gears. It remained as the classic Ferrari base of 7.87 ft. (2.40 m), which penalized comfort (always for two). The GTB debuted at the Paris Motor Show in 1964, and its aesthetic classicism, deemed excessive by the French critics, was revealed to be this model's trump card. Other French experts instead judged it to be exceptional and fiery, however, suitable only for expert drivers: stiff and with minimum roll, it tended to swivel around on itself, especially when not equipped with race tires. Due to these characteristics, it was rather difficult to drive, especially on bumpy roads.

92-93 Fabulous and very fast as in the best Maranello style, with its V12 engine of 201.36 cu. in. (3.3 liters) and 280 hp, the 275 GTB of 1964 was one of the most loved by the pure Ferrari fans. The car in the photo belonged to the first "wide-mouthed" series of 1964.

94-95 The racecar version of the 275 GTB exploited the robust mechanics' talent for speed and resistance.

TECHNICAL SPECIFICATIONS
275 GTB - GTB/4 (1964–1968)

Engine: 60° V12 cylinders

200.44 cu. in. (3,286 cc),
bores/stroke: 3.08" x 2.35" (77 x 58.8 mm)

3 Weber DCZ/6 twin carburetors or 6 Weber DCN 3

Power: 280 hp at 7,500 rpm
300 hp at 8,000 rpm (GTB/4)

Porsche synchronized 6-speed transmission

Tires: 205 x 14" 195 x 14"

Curb-weight: 2,420 lbs. (1,100 kg)

Length: 173" (4,325 mm)

Width: 69" (1,725 mm)

Height: 49.8" (1,245 mm)

Speed: from 159.96 to 165.5 (GTB/4) mph
(from 258 to 268 km/h)

Consumption: from 4.8 to 5.2 gal/62 mi
(from 18 to 20 l/100 km)

96-97 This Spider was presented at the Paris Motor Show in 1964. It was less powerful (260 hp) but was still an excellent example of the Italian style of the 1960s.

97 top The single-shaft 12-cylinder engines appeared with 3 or 6 twin carburetors.

However, during its three-year career, the GTB was given diverse aesthetic and mechanical modifications before the GTB/4, which boasted of four-cams, a racecar dry sump engine, and a set of six carburetors in order to reach 300 hp. Changes also came about on the propeller shaft, now housed in a stiff torque tube connected to the engine and transmission, which made this GTB/4 one of the most outstanding Ferrari cars, able to give a new look to Maranello productions. The GTB performed well also in the races, thanks to the care the Racing Division dedicated to this model, available with an all-aluminum chassis. Its sportive assets, particularly that of the GTB/4, were not underestimated by the dynamic United States importer, Luigi Chinetti, who had about 20 Spiders prepared, with the chassis made by Scaglietti. The GTB's story ended in 1968, also due to American limitations imposed in the *crash* and pollution tests. At the end of 1968 the GTB series reached an off-the-record number of 542 autos, a satisfactory figure all in all if compared to a total production estimated at 3,467 units. It was then replaced by another renowned Maranello sports car, the "Daytona."

98-99 *This very remarkable single-shaft engine with its six twin carburetors became a 4 camshaft engine.*

100-101 *The Berlinetta 275 GTB built in 1964 was one of the most important samples of Ferrari technology in the 1960s and represented a big leap forward, revealing astounding shapes and a V12 engine of 201.36 cu. in. (3.3 liters) and 280 hp with a 5-speed gearbox set separately at the rear wheel.*

Ferrari 250/330

Le Mans

On the road and racetracks

The line dividing the Grand Touring Ferrari road cars from the racing models was very subtle. This could be seen in the extraordinary 250 LM Berlinetta which had to replace the multi-winner GTO in the GT World Championship races in 1964. However, the car did not race in the year of its debut, since it was not constructed as part of the 100 prototypes according to the rules, and therefore had to enter the more difficult Sport category, battling with more specialized cars that were more powerful and designed only for races. It seemed that there were only 32 examples of the 250 LM. Subsequent to being beaten by "Regulations," it accomplished prestigious victories, such as that of the 24 Hours of Le Mans in 1965 and also in countless road races and on track. Other affirmations of prestige were highlighted in the luxury market, and due to its untiring 12 cylinders, it could circulate as a normal Grand Tourer and was always a protagonist in art auctions. Being a racecar, it was not expected to have the conveniences of a normal GT, but its fascination remained unchanged with time, even after 50 years, also because it was designed by an artist like Pininfarina and built by Scaglietti in aluminum sheets and fiberglass plastic parts. The 250 LM's line possessed a brutal fascination typical of a racing *supercar*, but already in 1965 Pininfarina had proposed 16 more "civilized" samples, with a more practical compartment, a panoramic rear window, air vents, supplementary slits on the top and new windows – all prototypes marketed in the USA by the usual, most skillful importer, Luigi Chinetti.

The bodywork was multi-tubular, weighing 173.8 lbs. (79 kg), and possessed modern, quadrilateral, oscillating suspensions. Substantially, this was a racecar configuration to be taken into account also in case of the most simple inspections of the mechanics: the enormous rear trunk took up more than half the car, even if made of fiberglass plastic, and to avoid any risks, you had to make sure it was well sustained upon opening.

The car itself underwent some modifications in its not too brief sports career, maintaining its typical features with the ever reliable V12 mid-engine, almost immediately upgraded in its engine displacement and power output (3.3 liters/320 hp instead of 3 liters/300 hp). On the road it appeared like a truly absolute Ferrari racecar – in reality it was the closed model (purchasable) of the 250 P prototype. One could immediately tell from its structure that it was created mainly for this purpose: it was a two-seater and did not avail of luggage room, since the tail could accommodate only a huge 15-inch (375 mm) spare tire. Also the interior finishing did not resemble a normal compartment that could alleviate the discomfort of those racing or traveling in such an extreme automobile. Only later did they realize that a racer – or even a simple driver – performed better if he was comfortable.

102-103 In 1962, the TRI 330 LM won the 24 Hours of Le Mans. It was the last Ferrari racecar with a frontal engine driven by Phil Hill and Olivier Gendebien.

104-105 and 105 The time had come to say goodbye also for this very powerful and fast TRI 330 LM with a front engine and 390 hp, which gave way to the updated 250 LM with a rear engine. The all-rear mechanics also included a great aluminum hood. Some also wanted a fiberglass chassis. The hefty V12 of 300-320 hp was set over a tubular chassis and weighed 1,804 lbs. (820 kg).

The dashboard was a very simple container for instruments, push-buttons and levers: aesthetics was not the foremost concern, since what mattered was to save weight to be able to stay within the required 1,760 lbs. (800 kg). However, the powerful roar of the 12 cylinders cancelled every perplexity and whoever took the wheel was seduced by the violence of the engine, and as in all the Maranello cars, it was the best part of the project design, even if its primary destination was racing competitions. The LM managed to excel even in "normal" usage since the driver had a full view of all his surroundings despite the fact that the compartment possessed few panes and big stiles, and he had to be prepared to make some extra effort to control the LM also when he wanted to push it harder than necessary. Therefore, it was other than an easy car, but very engrossing even for street driving. The disc brakes remained efficient if not pushed to the limit, but improved greatly in the ventilated disc version. In any case, the Le Mans always performed its duty, and even today is a *star* in all the historical motor shows.

106 and 107 This 330 shows a Le Mans type of setup with the air inlets for the frontal 4-liter engine. The front for the 298.99-cu. in. (4.9-liter) engine derived from the monobloc of the standard 400 SA, but with Testarossa elements. The special Le Mans bodywork was designed for top speeds and drew inspiration from the rear-engine 246 ST Sport of 1961.

108-109 The chassis of the TRI LM built at Fantuzzi's adopted aerodynamic solutions of that time, such as the clipped tail, transversal spoiler and big profiled roll bar, which acted as a flap with the huge windshield, as prescribed then.

Ferrari 330 GT 2+2

110-111 *On the successful model of the 330 GT, Pininfarina in 1966 achieved this gorgeous coupe for the Princess de Rethy. It was a good exercise for the future 365 of 1965, which retained the style line with an output of 320 hp.*

112-113 and 114-115 *The elegance of the Ferraris of the 1960s is confirmed by this classic two-seater coupe, 14.66 ft. (4.47 m) long, 5.41 ft. (1.65 m) wide and 4.19 ft. (1.28 m) high, with its V12, 268.48-cu. in. (4.4-liter) engine delivering 300 hp.*

Fast but comfortable

1964 was a very important year for Maranello – its racecars, from the 158 to the 250 LM and 250 GTO, had won all there was to win – Ferrari renovated its GT "commercial" sector and increased its production in 1963 (from 598 to 654), along with the staff (from 430 to 450). The models on the price list were the 275 GTB/GTS, the admiral 500 Superfast (for special markets) and especially this 330 GT 2+2, which replaced the successful 250 GT 2+2. It was less elegant than its predecessor but represented an important production sector; it cost 7.5 million lire, whereas the new Fiat 850 utility car was selling for 849,000 lire. It still bore the elegant Pininfarina style, but the insertion of the four headlights spoiled the classical elegance of its lines. Maranello also realized this and, despite the success of the first series (622 sold), took heed of the opinion of the most faithful Ferrari followers. In 1965, Maranello passed on to the more balanced and pleasant "second series" with a nose of only two headlights, light alloy wheels and other finishing touches, such as the air vents on the sides, enough to make the car assume a sportier look. It also became a more livable coupe, suitable to long and more comfortable trips, and easier to drive. The fundamental dimensions, compared to the 250 GT 2+2, increased in length: 193.6 in. (4,840 mm); width: 68.6 in. (1,715 mm); height: 54.4 in. (1,360 mm). Even the powerful Ferraris had to adapt themselves to market demands, mounting those accessories that made them more pleasant to drive: after the four overdrive gears, a reliable 5-speed gearbox was placed, and on request, also air-conditioning and power steering. The following were always requested: safety belts, head rests and electric crystals. These were not too spectacular perhaps, but they matched the car's class. The "two lights" of 1965 were simpler, surely more elegant, but the market for this model seemed to be saturated and the production of a second series reached the 468 figure out of a total of 1,090, which justified this model's commercial validity, produced for over three years in the renovated Maranello factory. The mounting was instead always entrusted to the Pininfarina factory in Grugliasco, which willingly accepted the prestigious assignment.

Still traditional mechanics

Typical Ferrari mechanics: driven by the V12, renovated in structure and engine displacement now at 241.98 cu. in. (3,967 cc) in the 400 Superamerica; it boasted 300 hp, or rather, about 25 more than the previous model. The engine-gear assembly was all in the front and also the suspensions (quadrilateral in front and rigid bridge at the back), following the typical Ferrari tradition. More important changes were found only on the short wheelbase 330 GTC - GTS of 1966. The improvements in the compartment were considerable and Ferrari himself, who used a 330 for his trips, gave the team some tips. In the end, the 330 turned out to be more livable than the previous one, with Connolly leather all over the compartment, wooden trim on the dashboard and also the air-conditioning option – quite a benefit for better onboard living. At the wheel, the clients were satisfied – even if experience and skill were not something everyone possessed – to be able to make the best of a quality engine that could push up to 138.88 mph (224 km/h) as clocked. Its power output, 300 hp, and weight, 3,036 lbs. (1,380 kg), counseled the less expert drivers to take a more cautious and rational approach if they did not want to face the rear axles' forceful reaction (moreover, self-locking) especially on wet roads.

TECHNICAL SPECIFICATIONS

330 GTC (1966–1968)

Engine: 60° V12 cylinders

241.98 cu. in. (3,967 cc),
bores/stroke: 3.08" x 2.84" (77 x 71 mm)

3 twin carburetors 40 DFI

Power: 300 hp at 7,000 rpm

4-speed transmission (later 5-speeds)

Tires: 210 x 14"

Length: 178.8" (4,470 mm)

Width: 68.4" (1,710 mm)

Height: 50.4" (1,260 mm)

Curb-weight: 3,036 lbs. (1,380 kg)

Speed: 151.9 mph (245 km/h)

Ferrari Dino 206

A historical leap forward

Though with some regret, Enzo Ferrari was ready for the big leap that meant moving on to the rear motor, a solution he practically was forced to adopt in Formula One since 1960 and in the Sport series, in order to remain competitive. In 1965, the "engineer," who until then had been faithful to the front engine/rear traction in his prestigious Grand Tourers, had to give in: the agreement with Fiat that year obliged him to build 500 V6 engines to be able to race also in Formula Two. This solution was finally concretized in a Grand Tourer of noteworthy qualities that debuted with the name "Dino" – a tribute to Ferrari's firstborn son, who had passed away at only 24 years of age. Pininfarina had anticipated in 1965 a two-seater mid-engine coupe that drew inspiration from the Ferrari Sport version, and refinished the new chassis with mastery, creating one of the most important two-seater Grand Tourers among his own productions. Its soft supple lines and "old style" aspects possessed such an aggressive appeal that it was almost impossible not to fall under its spell. Production effectively started in May 1968, almost two years after the sporty Fiat series with the same type of Ferrari motor, and was preceded by a series of prototypes that anticipated its definitive form. The first 100 Dino 206, as always built at Scaglietti's, first in aluminum, sold like hotcakes: it was difficult to resist the fascination of its lines that resembled the racecar, and it is still very attractive, 45 years later. With its very brilliant 6 cylinder/122 cu. in. (2-liter) engine, it met with some difficulty when compared to the Porsche 911S with its overhang rear engine. Though production was initially slow, given that this 122 cu. in. (2-liter) version was created in 1969, 152 cars were sold. After

practically being forced to increase in cylinders and output, in 1969 the Dino was much more appreciated by the Ferrari fans who, for the moment, did not fear comparison with the more established German sports cars, especially the mixed types. The new 146 cu. in. (2.4-liter) engine, remodeled in its internal measurements and with the three Weber carburetors, increased in output by 15 hp (now 195 hp at 7,600 rpm), and boasted of a considerable increase of the maximum torque which improved the elasticity of the 246's gears. The new 146 cu. in. (2,400 cc) version also changed in its exterior dimensions and increased the wheelbase from 91.2 in. to 93.6 in. (2,280 to 2,340 mm), thus improving livability features. It was longer by some .039 in. (10 cm), 169 in. (4,235 mm) instead of 166 in. (4,150 mm), while width and height remained invariable. Its weight increased notably from 1,980 lbs. (900 kg) of the 206 model in aluminum to 2,376 lbs. (1,080 kg) of the new version in steel.

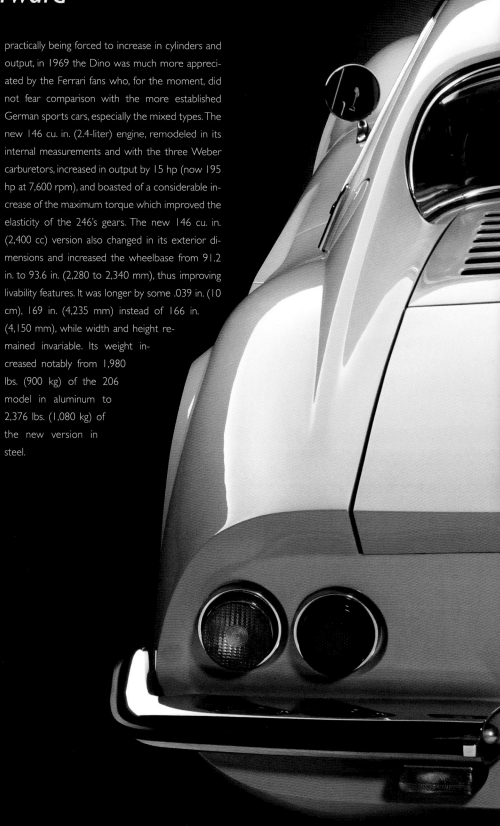

116-117 The Dino 206 represented an important step taken by Ferrari production with this "tiny" GT of 1967. The Maranello House introduced new construction concepts, not only regarding the rear engine but also new V6 cylinders, first with 122.04 cu. in. (2 liters) and then 146.44 cu. in. (2.4 liters) developed for the sporty Fiat models, with fantastic chassis for both versions.

118-119 The Dino design derived from the races, to offer an engine for the Formula Two and also for the small sport racing competitions, to battle with German and English rivals.

Small but rational

With tubular bodywork, there were a lot of options for structuring the compartment; the driver's seat and the sector-grid for the 5-speed gear lever really gave a sensation of being at the wheel of a racing prototype. The two seats slid lengthwise, upholstered on the sides, but could not recline, and the most frequently used commands scattered here and there on the dashboard could be activated with relative ease, whereas the steering wheel, small in diameter, made the steering maneuvers faster. The engine sprinted vigorously forward starting from 1800 revs, and on accelerating, the howl of the 6 cylinders behind the driver gave that thrill expected by whoever purchased such an extreme car. It offered indispensable performance typical of a purebred sports car, the behavior of which resembled (with due proportions) that of a racecar, and at most, required a lot of attention to avoid abrupt reactions. The American press had often compared it to its direct competitor, the Porsche 911, which was less expensive, better built and more livable, but a loser at the wheel, compared to the small Ferrari that could boast of better sports performance and superior precision. This basis from this starting point, Maranello's effort has always been to improve both product quality and drivability. In the span of eight years, production of the 206 totaled 3,913 units, with the clear prevalence of the "Berlinette" – almost double (2,487) compared to the "open" models (1,274).

120-121 With time, the lines of the Dino GTs reasserted their validity. Performance was almost the same as their rival's, the Porsche 911 S but offered a more sporty drive, the fruit of a more modern design and a 6-cylinder engine delivering 195 hp.

TECHNICAL SPECIFICATIONS

DINO 206 GT (1967)

Engine: 65° V6 cylinder central, transversal
121.81 cu. in. (1,997 cc),
bores/stroke: 3.44" x 2.28" (86 x 57 mm)
3 Weber twin carburetors 40 DCFN
Power: 180 hp at 8,000 rpm
5-speed transversal transmission

Tires: 185 x 14"
Wheelbase: 91.2" (2,280 mm)
Length: 166" (4,150 mm)
Width: 68" (1,700 mm)
Height: 46" (1,150 mm)
Curb-weight: 1,980 lbs. (900 kg)
Speed: 145.7 mph (235 km/h)
Consumption: 4.2 gal/62 mi (16 l/100 km)

Ferrari 365 GT 2+2

Relax, be comfortable!

Enzo Ferrari had never forgotten that particular coupe, at least in theory, and without losing sight of livability issues, he got down to working on the "family unit" coupe 2+2, which did not preclude the transport of more than two people and occupied a considerable slice of Maranello's production. Models like this 365 GT 2+2 of 1967 confirmed that Ferrari, on offering products of this kind, had once again proven his foresight. In 1972, this new type of coupe changed styles, following the new trends, which probably did not arouse enthusiasm in the more refined but remained on the Ferrari price list for many years. If the setting of its mechanics imitated that of its predecessor, its design followed other paths with respect to the preceding 365 GT 2+2. Its shape was no longer soft and roundish, but terse and marked, almost square. Many were astonished by these untraditional lines, but the commercial success of this model and its descendants up to 1992 confirmed that the new options hit the nail on the head. The

122-123 The 365 2+2 of 1967 practically ended the line of more classical 2+2 Ferraris, which were always welcomed abroad due to their dimensions, performance and abundant and roomy 2+2 seats.

124-125 Despite its size and weight, the 365 GT 2+2 could deliver 151.9 mph (245 km/h) with more than acceptable comfort, thanks to its servo steering, self-leveling suspension and disc brakes.

car, driven by the powerful 12 cylinders of 268.48 cu. in. (4.4 liters), could deliver 340 hp and be pushed up to 151.9 mph (245 km/h). Analyzing the body, it was noted that the wheelbase had increased by 1.95 in. (5 cm) compared to the previous version, to the full benefit of the passengers in the backseat, who now had more room for their legs and a more modern, trimmer compartment, more suitable to the traveling trends of the 1970s. Passengers got into two rear seats quite easily, inclining the backrests of the front seats with a simple lever, and then enjoyed the ample view, thanks to the abundance of glass panes and the thin stiles of the roof panel. The four seats, finished with care in Connolly leather, were among the most comfortable and well exploited, because of the greater volume the new design offered. The dashboard and the central console containing the instruments were also upholstered, lined, and matched with the finishing of the car, which in those times sold for 7 million lire. Also the floor exuded quality with moquette carpeting; the leather-type panels were good, with wooden inserts especially on the central console to satisfy the rich and extravagant American clients who looked not only for performance but above all for comfort at all levels. Even the trunk met the needs of the four passengers. Some Americans, however, complained of the lack of height due to the receding line of the roof panel. This 365 deeply satisfied the clients, especially those from the U.S.A., and remained unchanged until 1976. Some 576 were sold and replaced by stylistically similar models (the 400 and 412) but powered by 12 cylinders of 298.99 cu. in. (4.9 liters), and remained in production for 20 years – a sign of the popularity also of Ferraris of this type, enjoyed by a certain public (mostly Americans).

As the experts are well aware, Maranello had always treasured the experiences gained with all the preceding models, a legacy which very few companies in the world possessed. And so this 365 adopted the same technology as the 1967 version; it therefore had the 268.48 cu. in. (4.4 liter) engine of the 365 GT4, of the more evolved and refined type, with four overhead camshafts and the 2 × 3 Weber twin carburetors set between the camshafts, also to lower the line of the crankshaft. In this version the V12 delivered 340 hp, deemed sufficient for a coupe that weighed 3,300 lbs. (1,500 kg) and could hit a top speed of 151.0 mph (245 km/h). Even the chassis remained faithful to the Ferrari concepts, with elliptical tubes and some improvements. One detail again contributing to the good livability of this coupe was the broadening of the rear gauge. Other features were the four quadrilateral, independent wheels of the 365 Coupe and the Daytona, with an elastic system furnished by telescopic shock absorbers integrated with a stability corrector. It also had ventilated disc brakes, servo-assistance, and power steering, by then a must on this type of Ferrari, not designed for excessive sports performance.

TECHNICAL SPECIFICATIONS
365 GT 2+2 (1967–1972)
Engine: 60° V12 cylinders
267.79 cu. in. (4,390 cc),
bores/stroke: 3.24" x 2.84" (81 x 71 mm))
3 twin carburetors 40 DFI
Power: 300 hp at 7,000 rpm
4-speed transmission (later 5-speeds)
Tires: 210 x 14"
Curb-weight: about 3,256 lbs. (1,480 kg)
Length: 198.96" (4,974 mm)
Width: 71.44" (1,786 mm)
Height: 53.8" (1,345 mm)
Speed: 151.9 mph (245 km/h)

Ferrari 365 GTB4 Daytona

As beautiful as ever

At the end of the 1960s, sports cars started to change; racecars introduced new concepts, transforming the philosophy and aesthetics of road cars as well. This 365 GTB/4, called "Daytona" in memory of the prestigious victory at the 24 Hours of Daytona in 1967 (three Ferrari cars won the three top places) was a Grand Tourer, and though it did not negate Maranello's technical concepts, it had to face new and fierce rivals such as the fellow Italian Lamborghini Miura (mid-engine and 12 transversal cylinders of 250 hp). With its new line, however, designed by the new talents at Pininfarina's division, the Daytona synthesized the new trends well, even in its details. Precisely in 1968, Maranello produced 729 cars with 500 employees and presented its new coupe; the chassis boasted an extraordinary personality and a timeless elegance. As to style, the Daytona was somewhat like a tiny revolution because in some aspects, it moved away from the usual features: aerodynamics were dominant, the typical Ferrari grille disappeared and the headlights practically drowned in the hood. In the first 1968 series, a Plexiglas band completely covered the four lights, all assembled together in a splendid body shell 177 in. (4,425 mm) long, 70.4 in. (1,760 mm) wide and 49.8 in. (1,245 mm) tall. The chassis in steel sheets and the mobile parts in aluminum, as in the previous Berlinette, were always built by Scaglietti.

TECHNICAL SPECIFICATIONS
GTB4 (1968–1973)
Engine: 60°V12 cylinders
267.79 cu. in. (4,390 cc),
bores/stroke: 3.24" x 2.84" (81 x 71 mm)
6 Weber 20 twin carburetors 40 DCN
Power: 352 hp at 7,500 rpm
5-speed rear axle transmission
Tires: 215/70 x 15"
Length: 174" (4,425 mm)
Width: 69" (1,760 mm)
Height: 49.8" (1,245 mm)
Curb-weight: 2,640 lbs. (1,200 kg)
Speed: 173.6 mph (280 km/h)
Consumption: from 5.2 to 6.5 gal/62 mi
(from 20 to 25 l/100 km)

126-127 While the sporty rear mid-engine concept was starting to take hold, Ferrari remained on the classical side with its very powerful GTs with front engines: the splendid 365 GTB proposed the front-motor, rear-gearbox theme with independent wheel suspension.

128-129 The 365 GTB in 1971 changed its look and adopted pop-up headlights, also in view of the American market. The model was fascinating: 1,350 were produced in five years.

Technology at its utmost

In mechanics, the Ferrari designers started with components tested on other models, like the bodywork (275 GTB and 330 GTC) and the overhead four-cams engine (GTB/4) – an evolved and refined detail that was rarely adopted by the Ferraris of those times – and practically utilized the transaxle mechanics scheme of the 275 GTB with dry sump lubrication with 3.64 gal. (14 liters) of oil. The gearshift maintained its five speeds, positioned at the rear, just before the differential box. The bodywork, always in steel tubes as in the Ferrari tradition, was the basis on which the entire car was structured. The independent suspensions repeated the refined patterns already seen in some Ferrari models, but this new one was the most evolved

that Maranello had ever seen. And yet such a flawless line, which still excites Ferrari enthusiasts today, had to undergo modifications. So in 1971 the perspex band in front was removed and pop-up headlights were adopted, as in other sports cars of that period. The tail, short and clipped, remained the same and gave strength and sportiness to the entire car, which seemed to be one of the most successful Ferrari Grand Tourers, with an off-the-record production of 1,350 units – a noteworthy figure for a car of this class. The Spider version could not be missing in a similar sports series – though it was not easy to produce, given the technology of those times – but the Daytona did not present any problems, thanks to its robust coupe

chassis. The Daytona Spider, with the same dimensions as the coupe, debuted in a striking yellow at the Frankfurt Motor Show in 1969. The two-seat compartment did not feign luxury, but exhibited precise research for functionality in speed driving. From today's viewpoint, even with its canvas top rolled down, this Spider maintained a flawless elegance and aroused great interest: Maranello built only a few hundred of this open-shell version.

Though created as a Grand Tourer, the Daytona also obtained numerous sports victories, especially in the hands of the teams that had always handled Maranello's racing activities. The special prototypes with their chassis in aluminum and plastic (and output from 403 to 470 hp) competed in

130-131 and 131 top It was not easy to transform a coupe into a Spider, but in the case of the Daytona, the operation succeeded perfectly. The last Daytona to be produced in Maranello was a Spider. The cabin highlighted the typical settings of the time.

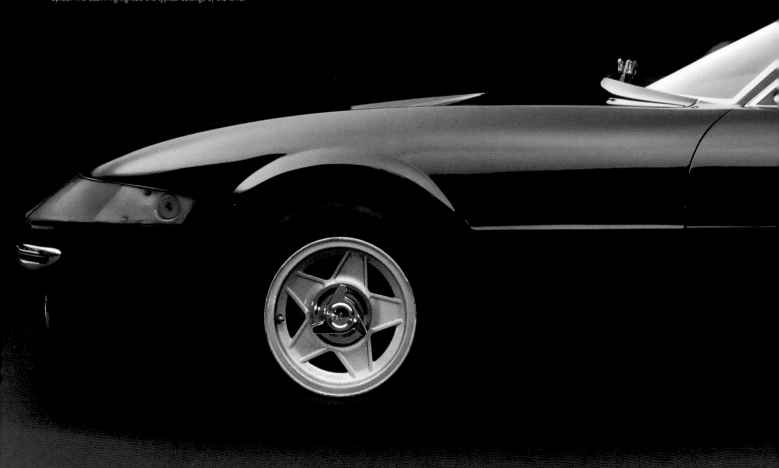

around 40 important international races up to 1979, with stylish wins in the 24 Hours of Le Mans, at Watkins Glen, at the Tour de France and at the 9 Hours of Kyalami in 1972. Also in 1973, 1974 and 1975 in the endurance races, the 365 GT/4 achieved victories in Daytona, Le Mans and even in the French Mountain championship where this Grand Tourer, despite its scarce agility, performed well at all times. Particularly spectacular was the victory achieved at the 24 Hours of Daytona in 1979, where a 365 GT/4 of two privateers came in as overall runners-up (five years after production had ended!). It was fantastic proof of the validity of a sports car that initially did not seem fit for racing.

The 1970s:

Hope Constrained by Austerity

THE 1960S HAD NURTURED SO MANY ILLUSIONS, WHEN ITALIANS WERE STILL TRAVELING WITH THEIR SMALL REAR-ENGINE UTILITY CARS BUT DREAMING OF BIGGER AND MORE COMFORTABLE ONES. IN DECEMBER 1973, HOWEVER, EVERYONE WAS JOLTED AWAKE BY GOVERNMENT PROVISIONS TO COUNTER THE PETROL CRISIS. THIS BROUGHT AN END TO EUPHORIA AND TRIGGERED A WAVE OF AUSTERITY. BUT NOW THEY COULD AT LEAST STILL AFFORD FOREIGN UTILITY CARS. THE FRONT-WHEEL DRIVE OF THE FIAT DOMINATED, AND THE BIGGEST SELLERS WERE THE 128 AND THE 127 (THE MOST POPULAR WITH OVER 1.8 MILLION UNITS), WHICH EUROPE ENVIED, COPIED AND BOUGHT. THEN CAME THE LANCIA 2000, THE REFINED FULVIA, THE LAMBORGHINI JARAMA AND THE ALFASUD, AN UNACKNOWLEDGED HOPE FOR ITALY'S SOUTHERN REGION. DURING THIS PERIOD, THE FIRST FOREIGN CAR SOLD WAS THE RENAULT 5 (ABOUT A SIXTH OF THE NUMBER OF 127S SOLD). THE FERRARI, A MANUFACTURING FIRM BUT ALSO A FLAGSHIP, BATTLED STRENUOUSLY WITH THE ENGLISH AND THE GERMANS. OVER THIS 10-YEAR PERIOD IT WON THREE IRIDESCENT F1 TITLES AND COULD WELL BE SATISFIED. ITS PRODUCTION LEAPED FORWARD AND IN 1979 HAD DOUBLED TO 2,221 UNITS AND OFFERED FLEET ADMIRALS SUCH AS THE BB, BUT ALSO THE "TINY" 308. BY THEN FERRARI WAS MOVING WITHIN THE FIAT CIRCLES, BUT THE ENGINEER AND FOUNDER WAS ALWAYS AT THE HELM.

Ferrari 308 GTB

The turning point of the "tiny" ones

The celebrations for the brand's upcoming 30th anniversary were approaching and were by then a world event. The founder had not forgotten even the "tiny" ones named after his son, Alfredo (just like his father), which also reaped success from 1967 onward, despite the fact that this name was not familiar to the great public (they could not bear the Ferrari badge since this would have obliged them to have the 12-cylinder engines). In 1973, also due to the urging of the clientele and car dealers, the decision was made to promote these cars, "rechristening" them precisely with the Ferrari trademark. The Berlinetta 308 GTB, born two years after the four-seater coupe of 1973, synthesized the progress of these "tiny" ones: its engine became a V8 cylinder (instead of 6), then the bodywork and substantially all the mechanics became fundamental for the Ferrari evolution. The 308 GTB was crowned by success, with over 12,000 cars sold in 10 years. The Berlinetta was presented at the Paris Motor Show in 1975, when the Ferrari was getting ready to win its seventh Formula One world title. The line offered a comeback of some stylistic motifs already seen on the Ferrari Pininfarina cars, and the lines now became more determined, sharper, compared to the sweeping curves of the previous models. At the tail, the car maintained its rear-rigging stiles with the air vents. The choice of material, however, turned out to be impractical and after 712 autos in glass-reinforced plastic Scaglietti-style, the bodywork switched to a steel shell with 2,185 steel versions weighing 220-286 lbs. (100-130 kg) more. Two years later, the car was put side by side with the "convertible-top" versions. The evolution concentrated on a body 169 in. (4,230 mm) long, 0.2 in. (5 mm) less compared to the 6-cylinder Dino with over 12,000 units sold in 10 years, before the arrival of its substitute, the 348, in 1989.

This rational two-seater exploited the slightly bigger area offered by the new seats; however, the wheelbase remained the same at 93.6 in. (2,340 mm). Efforts were concentrated above all on the sporty position of the driver's seat, which allowed for adequate, comfortable and functional seating, thanks to the steering wheel that was adjustable in height, and the layout of the backrest and seat base. The analog instruments inserted on the dashboard in front of the driver were very clear, whereas the command levers were shifted to the central console and thus not easily triggered when driving, like the radio. The boot benefitted from the adjacent transversal engine-gear box with a 14,644.8 cu. in. (240-liter) capacity. The shaft was accessible, though not really insulated from the heat of the adjacent engine: it could be reached by lifting the cover without the practical air springs. The front contained only the radiators and spare tire. A sporting car in line with the times, brilliant up to a certain extent, fast and exciting behind the wheel, it then became a model to be handled only by experts because of its sudden, very fast reactions, which progressively diminished in the following series. Its sporty spirit and rather bizarre oversteering, however, achieved great success even abroad.

Its technology took roots in the 6-cylinder Dino of the 1960s, but the mechanical components were different and more advanced, starting with the motor, which became a 90° V8 cylinder with dry sump ("30" was the engine displacement whereas "8" stood for the number of cylinders), with four overhead camshafts driven by a toothed belt. The power supply was also renovated; in 1980 it was delivered by mechanical injection (it lost about 40 hp). Then in 1982, with the four valves per cylinder, a bit of power and elasticity were restored (reaching 240 hp). On the chassis, a metallic tubular lattice and double-wishbone independent suspensions with coil springs were mounted, with an anti-roll bar and telescopic dampers. It had, of course, rack steering. The gearbox formed a unit with the engine and was thus transversal, and had a 5-speed transmission with self-locking differential. Total weight was 2,398 lbs. (1,090 kg), whereas the first examples in fiberglass plastic saved up to 220-286 lbs. (100-130 kg).

TECHNICAL SPECIFICATIONS

308 GTB (1975)

Engine: 90° V8 central, transversal

178.54 cu. in. (2,927 cc),
bores/stroke: 3.24" x 2.84" (81 x 71 mm)

4 twin carburetors 40 DCNF, later mechanic injection

Power: 255 hp at 7,700 rpm

5-speed transmission

Tires: 205/70 VR14"

Wheelbase: 98.4" (2,500 mm)

Length: 163.6" (4,090 mm)

Width: 68" (1,700 mm)

Height: 44.8" (1,120 mm)

Curb-weight: 2,398 lbs. (1,090 kg)

Speed: 156.24 mph (252 km/h)

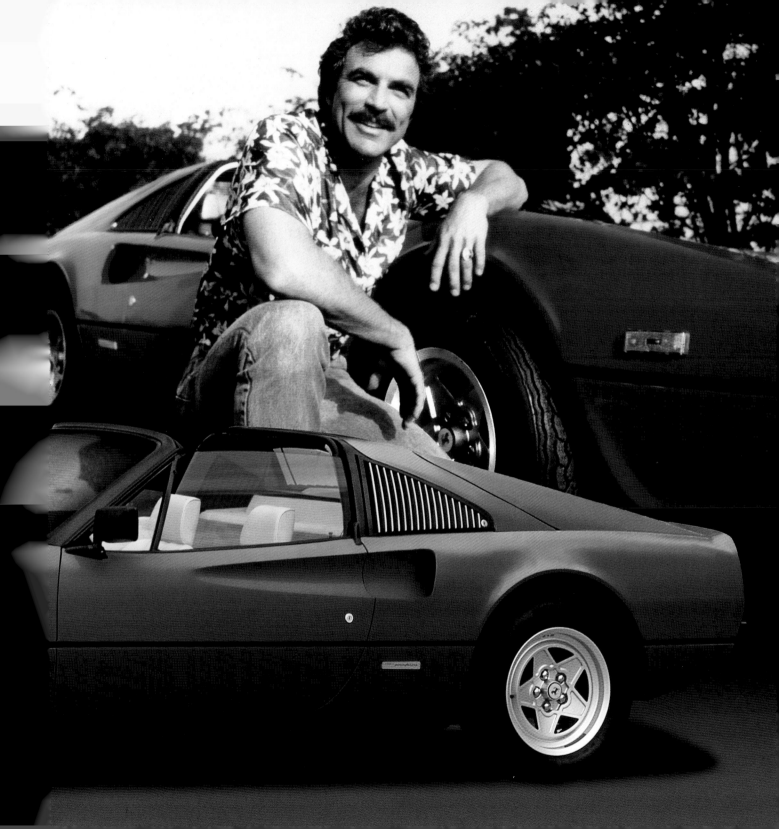

Ferrari 512 BB

In the front line for 20 years

1973: Maranello's super sports car, the 365 BB, Berlinetta Boxer, already had its fans who were greatly attracted to the new, rear-engine supercars, and could afford to possess a car with these features at such a price (85 million lire). In 1976, when the 1,600 Ferrari employees produced 2,565 cars, the 365 GT/4 BB changed its name (to 512 BB), engine, aesthetics (only partly) and measurements: it was 1.56 in. (4 cm) longer, larger by 3.12 in. (8 cm) and had a bigger and more powerful engine – a 305.1 cu. in. (5-liter) displacement with 12 flat cylinders (thus the name, 512) – and weighed 3,080 lbs. (1,400 kg) in-

stead of the 2,464 lbs. (1,120 kg) of the first 365 GT/4 BB. It maintained the displacement of four overhead camshafts and the vertical Weber 40 IF3C twin carburetors, replaced two years later by Bosch indirect injection, more suitable to the characteristics of the BB and to the new circulation. Injection enhanced the handling capacity, but it lost a bit in pure output, passing from 380 hp at 7,700 rpm of the 365 GT/4 BB to the current 360 hp at 6,800 rpm with the speed of 186 mph (300 km/h) decreased by 2. The structure had the same layout as the mid-engine 365 BB, the original V12 with cylinders laid out flat in

two opposite banks and the 5-speed gearbox under the engine, which allowed the 512 BB a compact wheelbase of 100 in. (2,500 mm) and length of 174.4 in. (4,360 mm), 1.56 in. more (4 cm); the car was also a bit wider, with bigger rear tires. As to the bodywork, Pininfarina kept a design that resembled the compact cars of Maranello more than the great Ferrari 12 cylinders. Its line, however, would leave its mark for the next 20 years and adapt itself well to the variants of the model's mechanics. The 512 BB of 1976 remained in production for six years before it was replaced by the fuel-injection 512 BBi.

138-139 The 512 BB was the 1976 evolution of the BB (Berlinetta Boxer) series. Its exclusive "flat" engine (with 180° V12 cylinders) then delivered 360 hp. The Berlinetta shown here was slightly changed at the tail with aerodynamic flaps. It lasted 20 years with Bosch fuel injection and lateral radiators.

140-141 The 512 BB's huge and heavy aerated rear trunk was later modified. It opened completely to allow access to the hefty engine-gearbox unit.

In 1981 the "Boxer" formula had already been withdrawn from Formula One, taken over by single-seater turbos such as the 126 C of Maranello. But in the Grand Touring sector, the scheme of 12 cylinders on two opposite banks still confirmed its validity and the favor of the more faithful Ferrari enthusiasts. The 512 BB was a proof of this: it practically had the same basic technical setting as the previous BB and consolidated its success, resulting in 240 units sold in 1980. And it still promised a long life since the "Boxer" formula would remain in production until 1996, when Maranello produced the 550 Maranello with a more traditional scheme, front engine and rear gearbox. Even if the succeeding versions kept the same technical setting, the 512 was the last to bear the name BB, Berlinetta Boxer. The novelty of the 512 BBi of 1981 consisted of Bosch K-Jetronic fuel injection, which was more regular at full speed, and ensured that indispensable function in the new type of traffic. Even in its design, the 512 BB remained more on the classic side, with the large grille for the radiator still in front. It was difficult, however, to distinguish it from the previous version, having maintained the same

setting and style lines. As a whole, with its particular engrossing air, it was welcomed by all and offered some peculiar detail such as the front spoiler, hardly notable but improving the grip at high speeds. The chassis in steel sheets, built by Pininfarina, favored the handling but did not lighten the car, which then reached 3,313.2 lbs. (1,506 kg) at curb weight. The transition to aluminum would come about only later, with the Testarossa of 1984, and would gain greater aesthetics, thanks to the water radiators and the now lateral air inlets at the height of the driver. The dimensions remained compact as in the Maranello Grand Tourers with the same "Boxer" mechanics: length of 176 in. (4.400 mm), width of 73.2 in. (1,830 mm) and height of 44.8 in. (1,120 mm). And what was it like at the steering wheel? The Argentine, Carlos Reutemann, at the end of 1981, affirmed the excellence of the engine and performance, exploitable at 65 percent, with a very determined oversteer and brakes, which in sporty driving tended to tire out under stress. In about 12 years roughly 2,000 of the 512 BBs were produced with a slight prevalence of the injection versions.

TECHNICAL SPECIFICATIONS
512 BB (1976)

Engine: 180° V12 cylinders central, aluminum
301.52 cu. in. (4,943 cc)
bores/stroke: 3.28" x 3.12" (82 x 78 mm)
4 overhead camshafts with toothed belt
2 valves per cylinder
4 Weber 40 IF3C carburetors (since 1981, 512 BBi with K-Jetronic injection)
Power: 360 hp at 6,800 rpm
5-speed transmission
Tires: 215/70 VR 15" (front), 225/70 VR 15" (rear)
Length: 173" (4,400 mm)
Width: 72" (1,830 mm)
Height: 44.8" (1,120 mm)
Curb-weight: 3,087 lbs. (1,400 kg)
Speed: 187.24 mph (302 km/h)

142-143 The picture shows the refined flat 12-cylinder engine of the 512 BB (360 hp at 6,800 rpm) still powered by twin-choke carburetors, later replaced by indirect injection.

The 1980s:

An Increasing Decade

GENERAL CRISES, SOCIAL TENSIONS AND THE SECOND PETROL SHOCK HAD OBLIGED THE AUTO INDUSTRY TO REVIEW

ITS PLANS AND PROJECTS IN ORDER TO REDUCE CONSUMPTION AND TRY TO BOOST PERFORMANCE, DESPITE ALL THE LIMI-

TATIONS: PETROLEUM AT THE START OF THE DECADE COST 10 DOLLARS PER DRUM, BUT DUE TO THE VARIOUS CRISES, IN

1979 IT HIT THE 20-DOLLAR MARK. HOWEVER, ALL BUILDERS, EVEN OF THE TOP CARS, HAD TO FACE NEW CHALLENGES WITH

THE INJECTION SYSTEMS (PRACTICALLY OBLIGATORY IN THE FOLLOWING YEARS), TO REDUCE CONSUMPTION AND DECREASE

POLLUTION. ELECTRONICS WERE A HELP IN OVERCOMING THE SAFETY AND EMISSION RESTRICTIONS, WHILE THE COMPUT-

ER WAS PROCLAIMED THE "PROTAGONIST" OF THE DECADE. THE FERRARI BEHAVED QUITE WELL IN FORMULA ONE AND

WON TWO WORLD TITLES. BUT EVENTS ABROAD COULD NOT BE IGNORED, GIVEN THAT FERRARI'S PRODUCTION DEPENDED

A LOT ON EXPORTS TO THE RICHER COUNTRIES. HOWEVER, IT MAINTAINED ITS 2-LITER MODELS TO AVOID TAXES ON EN-

GINE DISPLACEMENT, AND ANNUAL PRODUCTION OVER THE DECADE INCREASED GREATLY, FROM 2,470 TO 3,821 UNITS, UN-

DER GIOVANNI BATTISTA RAZELLI, THE GENERAL DIRECTOR SINCE 1985. THE MONDIAL 8 AND 288 GTO MADE THEIR DE-

BUTS. THE TESTAROSSA, 512 TR, 328, 348, 412, GTB TURBO, REMARKABLE F40, MONDIAL T AND 348 WERE MODELS THAT TES-

TIFIED TO MARANELLO'S VITALITY, EVEN IN SUCH DIFFICULT TIMES. UNFORTUNATELY, HOWEVER, ON AUGUST 14, 1988, ENZO

FERRARI PASSED AWAY AT THE AGE OF 90.

Ferrari Mondial 8

Many consider it the "back side" of the Ferrari, since its soft line, minimum determination and smooth surface did not make it seem to be a 155 mph (250 km/h) sports car but rather a calm coupe, almost a family car. In reality this was not so. Ferrari had conceived it especially for the American market, which gave it a warmer welcome than it did for the equivalent model 308 GT4 (aka "Dino"). First, he switched body makers, passing from Bertone to the trusted Pininfarina. The name Mondial came from Ferrari's historic racecars of the 1950s. This four-seater was a harmonic succession of surfaces and volumes that adapted to the distribution of the "all-rear" mechanics and to the size of the cabin, also considering the difficulties of designing a four-seater with a rear motor. The lines revealed a good harmony, despite the volumes shifted forward, and the cabin, which could easily be adapted and transformed into a cabriolet coupe, particularly satisfied the Californian drivers. Compared to the previous Pininfarina coupe, it gained 3.9 in. (10 cm) in its wheelbase, which was important to improve adaptability and make the car sleeker and gain prominence with an overall length of over 14.76 ft. (4.5 m). Its shape, squared in front (as for the Berlinette 308), became softer, lightened by the engine air inlets, with the light but robust, elongated roof line (an exclusive feature of the Pininfarina coupe), with the compact tail, favored by transversal mechanics, and with a sufficiently spacious trunk of 18,306 cu. in. (300 liters). This model did not draw so much interest from the more passionate Ferrari fans but it gained popularity abroad with a great number of clients who wished to travel fast and comfortably. Maranello took all the features into account, besides the power steering and the adoption of dampers regulated by a control panel, which controlled its calibration to heighten performance.

The Mondial 8 seemed to be almost created on purpose for the American market, aided by the Ferrari name and Chinetti's precious work. Livability was considered satisfying – or at least the American journalists believed so, though they mainly checked performance. The peculiarity of the Mondial was the practicality of four seats: if the two passengers in front were quite comfortable even with the sporty drive, this could not be said for those in the back, who had just enough legroom, and those who were tall were crammed into an unnatural position. To compensate, the compartment was elegant, with well-profiled adjustable seats (the front seats with reclining backs) and a steering wheel that could be set manually, in line with the trend of the '80s. It had squared lines and straight surfaces, the instruments rationally inserted on the great dash panel in front of the driver and the central *console* with the gear-shift command grid. The important U.S. magazine "Motor Trend" complained of the insufficient lateral resistance of the driver's seat, though it praised all the other functional characteristics, which justified the success it achieved in the States for almost 15 years. A few hundred cars were sold yearly, even when in 1989 the new T version arrived, almost unchanged in terms of design but with a longitudinal instead of transversal motor (and with 300 hp in place of the first version's 214). The Americans complained above all about the lack of power steering (which was added on the Mondial T in 1989), the inadequate air-conditioning for the temperature of the compartment, and certain design details. However, they were satisfied by the livability, braking stability, car usability for all situations, and the trunk. Ultimately, the car had all the qualities to establish its credentials on the American up-market, and in the 15-year production of this model (in four basic versions), the Maranello team obviously tried to improve it and eliminate the slight defects. 1993 saw the definitive closure of the chapter regarding this four-seater rear engine model, later replaced by the more traditional 456.

46-147 The Mondial 8 was an important event for Maranello: the chassis 2+2 was then achieved by Pininfarina with the very reassuring style of those times. Volumes were shifted forward to leave more room to the compartment, which was also used for the 1980 cabriolet. It was initially built with a 183.06-cu. in. (3-liter) engine of 214 hp and later upgraded to reach 270 hp.

48-149 This was the typical Pininfarina nose in the 1970s: with a negative lift profiling, pop-up headlights and air vents on the hood.

TECHNICAL SPECIFICATIONS
MONDIAL 8 (1989)

Engine: 90° V8 cylinders central, transversal
178.48 cu. in. (2,926 cc),
bores/stroke: 3.24" x 2.84" (81 x 71 mm)
Bosch electronic injection
Power: 214 hp at 6,600 rpm
transversal 5-speed transmission
Tires: 240/55 VR 390
Wheelbase: 106" (2,650 mm)
Length: 183.2" (4,580 mm)
Width: 71.6" (1,790 mm)
Height: 50" (1,250 mm)
Curb-weight: 3,179 lbs. (1,445 kg)
Speed: 142.6 mph (230 km/h)

Ferrari Testarossa

An astounding Berlinetta

When this Testarossa debuted at the Paris Motor Show in 1984, none of the Ferrari fans were surprised. Since its forerunner (the 365 GT4 BB) had appeared 13 years earlier, the manufacturing formula for this powerful Berlinetta was well known: a mid-engine driven by the exclusive 12 "Boxer" cylinders, inspired by the F1 races of the 1970s. The name, in keeping with Ferrari's custom of commemorating the past, recalled the famous Sport series, which triumphed in the world championships up to 1958, with red-coated engines exactly like that of this distant heir. The Grand Tourer presented in Paris had big ambitions in the sector since it represented the most advanced concept of the BB presented 13 years earlier. Its concept remained the same, but the car changed under all aspects, its chassis was overhauled for aerodynamics, its sides were given more dynamic lines, the big radiators had a new site and the air intakes were underscored by five streaks showing lateral air flow. The Testarossa revitalized the particular technological formula that had remained in production for 10 years, up to the arrival of the F512 M, the last Ferrari with the increase of 1.95 in. (5 cm) for more cabin room. Still for only two passengers, it now boasted a new front shaft of 9,153 cu. in. (150 liters) with the addition of the rear seats that could carry a pair of suitcases or a golf bag. The dimensions had not changed much: it was less than 14.76 ft. (4.5 m) long and almost 6.56 ft. (2 m) wide. Comfort and livability in the compartment improved due to the absence of cooling ducts, a motif repeated on the descendants of the same series (512 TR and F512 M) as well as on the compact Ferrari models of that period. The building of the aluminum body was not assigned to Scaglietti, but to Pininfarina, who ensured a high quality finishing.

150-151 *The Testarossa of 1984 was a logical evolution of the BB of 1973, of which 2,393 units were produced. It mounted an injection 12-cylinder "Boxer" 298.99-cu. in. (4.9-liter) engine of 390 hp and a top speed of 179.8 mph (290 km/h).*

152-153 *The Spider maintained its determined personality also at the rear, with wide engine cooling slits and long roof stiles that stretched out to the tail.*

Improved technology

There were no substantial changes with respect to the 1971 BB, but many variants to improve functionality and behavior. The "Boxer" with toothed belts was about 44 lbs. (20 kilos) lighter, and the engine output increased compared to the BB from 267.79 to 301.52 cu. in. (4,390 to 4,943 cc), with four valves per cylinder, gaining around 10 hp and giving greater elasticity to gearshifts (maximum torque 10 percent more) and a higher speed (179.8 mph – 290 km/h). Now the power supply was delivered through Bosch mechanical injection, which guaranteed greater gearshift fluidity, very much ap-

preciated by clients. The multitubular chassis had a central body, enhanced comfort and stability, four-sided deformable suspensions with anti-roll bars and telescopic dampers, double at the rear with disc brakes on the four tires but without ABS or servo control. The Ferrari technicians achieved an important victory with the Testarossa, and obtained approval for the very important U.S. market. The Testarossa's success was immediate: delivery times were extended to about two years on the waiting list! It also seemed that by 1984 more than 100 cars had been built, contributing to the relative success of

this model and its derivatives produced in 1966 with the arrival of the more traditional and very fast Berlinetta (such as the 550 Maranello). Whoever bought a Testarossa could count on standard air-conditioning, an adjustable steering column and seat and a high, electrically adjustable rear-view mirror. What were missing, as in other contemporary top cars, were the electrically adjustable seats, ABS, traction control, onboard computer and airbags. Notwithstanding all these, it was an absolutely unique and thrilling car for sportsmen, and hit a top speed of 180.42 mph (291 km/h)! Accelerating

154-155 A typical extreme Berlinetta, the Testarossa was exceptionally also produced as a Spider. A silver one was made for Gianni Agnelli and a black one for driver Olivier Gendebien. The mechanics remained the same over a length of 14.69 ft. (4.48 m).

took a little less than 15 seconds, but demanded attention since at times sudden oversteering occurred and was not easy to control. Steering at low speed was tiring, almost like taming a "monster" of almost 400 hp, with 55 percent of its weight on the rear axle. It was a car for a chosen few, and a really limited few when pushed to its limits. Driving it was an amazing experience and not suitable to wet roads, since the electronic control "sentinels" were still nonexistent. Furthermore, this was the last "grand" mid-engine Ferrari that remained in production.

TECHNICAL SPECIFICATIONS
TESTAROSSA (1973–1976)
Engine: 180° V12 cylinders central
301.52 cu. in. (4,943 cc),
bores/stroke: 3.28" x 3.12" (82 x 78 mm)
4 overhead camshafts with toothed belt
4 valves per cylinder
Power: 390 hp at 7,500 rpm
5-speed transmission
Tires: 225/50 VR 16" (front), 255/50 VR 16" (rear)
4 ventilated disc brakes
Wheelbase: 100" (2,550 mm)
Speed: 177.94 mph (287 km/h)
Length: 177" (4,485 mm)
Width: 79.04" (1,976 mm)
Height: 45.2" (1,130 mm)
Curb-weight: 3,320 lbs. (1,506 kg)
Speed: 180 mph (290 km/h)

Ferrari 288 GTO

Red fury

1984 seemed to be a golden year for the Prancing Horse: the 126 C4 possessed all the requirements to reconquer the F1 World Championship after a decade, but it was not so (Michele Alboreto made fourth place). The Testarossa was the top-of-the-line model of a production that counted almost 3,000 cars yearly. The 288 GTO (the numbers refer to engine displacement and number of cylinders, whereas "GTO" recalled the unbeatable GT of the prior 20 years). It had an aggressive line and above all a twin-turbo mechanics that anticipated by three years another exclusive Maranello top car, the F40 of 1987. The new car

was initially built in limited numbers, but then, given the orders, 272 cars were produced. Built for racing, its performance was amazing over 186 mph (300 km/h), and it became the magnificent road-legal sports car everyone remembers even today. One of its designers, Engineer Materazzi, recalls that the GTO came to light in 1992, when Ferrari himself strongly demanded an "absolutely non-middle-class sports car." To save time and money, they thought of a turbo, or rather, a twin-turbo which, however, used components already in production. The starting point was the 8 cylinders of the 308 GTB with four valves per cylinder, later used

also for the Lancia LC2, which could deliver 400 hp with the right modifications. The design was substantially the same, even if some details changed, especially in the aerodynamically modified rear end, where lateral slits appeared, including a clipped tail with a flashy spoiler and a total cooling grille on the engine lid. The result: an aggressive Berlinetta, 2.34 in. (6 cm) longer compared to the 120 in. (308 cm), but wider by 7.8 in. (20 cm). Available only in red, it soon reached the 200 target (of which 60 sold in the U.S.A., 45 in Italy and the remaining in the rest of the world), but the requests were so urgent that Maranello decided to raise the final number

TECHNICAL SPECIFICATIONS
288 GTO (1984)

Engine: 90° V8 cylinders central, longitudinal

174.15 cu. in. (2,855 cc),
bores/stroke: 3.2" x 2.84" (80 x 71 mm)

Weber Marelli direct injection twin turbo IHI

Power: 400 hp at 7,000 rpm

longitudinal 5-speed transmission
with self-lock differential

Tires: 225/55 VR16" (front), 265/50 VR16" (rear)

Wheelbase: 98" (2,450 mm)

Curb-weight: 2,552 lbs. (1,160 kg)

Length: 171.6" (4,290 mm)

Width: 76.4" (1,910 mm)

Height: 44.8" (1,120 mm)

Speed: 189.1 mph (305 km/h)

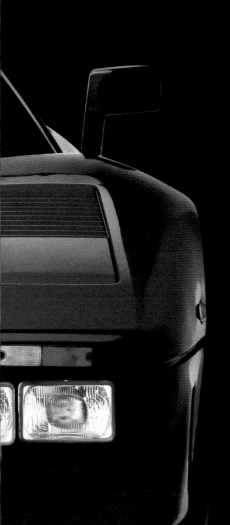

to 272. The success of the Grand Touring extreme sports car such as the 288 GTO pushed Ferrari to conceive a super sports car of this type also in the future. The GTO thus maintained the "sporty" and "family" feeling of the 308, with few elements distinguishing it from the original -- the bigger *spoiler* at the back and the rear-view mirrors up high.

The cabin also maintained that simple and essential air, in line with the features of the very fast Berlinetta designed for racing competitions. It stood out for its characteristic style lines, like the dashboard, upholstered in suede fabric; the non-adjustable steering wheel; and the sporty, sliding and very well-groomed seats, with a profiling that provided a firm road hold when taking the bends. The driver took a typical racing position in the seat (with headrest), which could be adjusted to tilt back. The main instruments were set on the small dash panel in front of the driver, whereas others were on the console between the seats with a series of commands such as the gearstick in a normal sector grid, besides the push-buttons and small levers for the heating system and the electric winding panes. There was also a touch of the "old style" like the starter pushbutton. There was practically no room for luggage, since the front shaft was occupied by the spare tire and there was no room behind the seats, not even for a big duffel bag. The GTO

certainly was not meant to be a comfortable GT, but rather, it had to relay the precise sensations (and a bit of discomfort) of a racecar, really a unique one for that 1980 period. The car was agile also in road traffic, with its 400 hp and weight of 2,552 lbs. (1,160 kg). You did not need much to realize that you had something really special and also very demanding in your hands: it was pure, wild and free from electronics that could tame the devastating power of its 400 hp and of the small Japanese turbines, with those overwhelming "sounds" in the compartment which were even enjoyable to the more sportive drivers. In this sense the GTO was a transition phase for the Maranello Gran Turismo, and it was really amazing how even on such an extreme sports car, and with so many horsepower ready to respond on the instant, the driving was so pleasant for those who could afford it – not only in terms of its price. Its really extraordinary qualities will be found, overhauled of course, in the sensational F40 of 1987. The GTO benefits would once again emerge in the racing models that performed really well. Ferrari studied the improvements needed to lighten the bodywork and achieve the utmost rigidity indispensable in a racecar. There was even a GTO Evolution that could deliver an output of 680 hp and a grip at the desired speeds, thanks to the rear flaps.

156-157 A sensational fireball also on the road with its V8 twin turbochargers of 400 hp and a speed of over 186 mph (300 km/h). The 288 GTO, built with composite materials, was an extremely long, (14.10 ft. – 4.3 m) two-seater racecar with light and essential setups for road use.

158-159 and 159 The 288 GTO immediately won the favor of the more demanding Ferrari faithful because of its performance and good handling. The lines provided for air inlets and relevant vents in the front and rear. A total of 272 units were built (more than planned).

Ferrari F40

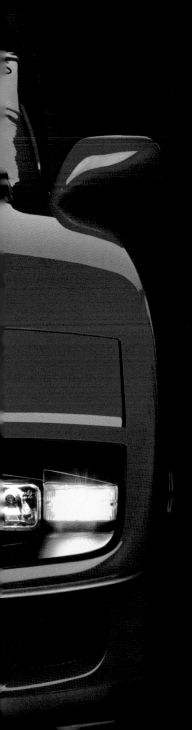

Built in 1987, this fantastic Grand Tourer was a step in the evolution of the Ferrari supercars, celebrating the epic story of the turbocharger, protagonist not only in Formula One, but also in mass production. Ferrari himself commissioned it after the positive experience of the 288 GTO; he wished for an even more extreme car but one that would set a new trend, whether or not the current production was exploited. His engineers presented him with a model that broke away from the past and gave indications for the future. So on the 40th anniversary of the house, this project was fulfilled (F40 was in fact an acronym for 40 years of Ferrari). It was one of the most innovative cars produced by Maranello, with 478 hp (to think that the "'engineer" would have wanted at least 500) and a speed of 200 mph (324 km/h). Initially intended for limited production, it upset the forecasts and by far exceeded the 1,000 target, becoming the forbidden dream of sports enthusiasts and car collectors all over the world, and was even the object of speculation on the market. During this period, the company was already a true and proper industry that produced 3,902 cars yearly with 1,773 employees. If the engines had started off with 8 cylinders, completely overhauled and transformed with the adoption of two Japanese turbochargers, the rest was the fruit of long research on structures, materials, aerodynamics and Formula One technology transfers to production. The result: a "Berlinetta" still designed by Pininfarina, a constant in the evolution of the Ferrari and sports cars in general. The F40's dominant feature was its big rear flap, forcing down and stabilizing at high speeds, ensuring ground transfer of its excessive output and also proving the accuracy of aerodynamics research on the car's flat underbody, which achieved a "ground effect" decisive for the car's grip and stability, thanks to the depression created. The dimensions of the F40 were quite compact: 71.6" (4,358 mm) long and 77.5' (1,970 mm) wide. It was defined as an "exceptional car" by all those who had worked on it and who had been given a free hand in defining its solutions. Designed and built in just 13 months with two other prototypes presented in July 1987, here was a "road legal" racecar, a global sports car, defined in its smallest details. Its chassis, for example, was built with composite materials such as carbon fiber, aluminum and Kevlar *honeycomb* panels, and with lightweight materials and magnesium, crucial to limit its weight to 2,420 lbs. (1,100 kg).

It was also a commercial success. Production, calculated at 1.5 cars a day, accelerated to three time that amount.

True sports cars were not meant to be comfortable, but the aim was to put the driver at ease stripping down all installations and accessories to the minimum. The compartment, therefore, was simple and without concessions, with black finishing and instruments scattered around like the various controls. The driver's seat was a well-profiled and comfortable racer seat, sliding with a fixed backrest and a steering wheel that allowed for an almost perfect drive, and a wide adjustable pedal in a light alloy. There was a start-up for races (push-button) along with winding crystal panes and air-conditioning. Luggage room was scarce, almost null, with a front sump. The spare tire was not provided but an emergency fire extinguisher was available.

160-161 The F40 immediately became a cult for automobile enthusiasts: it benefitted from the experience carried over from 288 GTOs overhauled to maximum power, with a Pininfarina chassis in composite materials and evolved aerodynamics synthesized in the great, fixed rear flap.

162-163 The design of the F40 was that of 1986, after the success of the 288 GTO with the mid-engine V8 twin turbochargers. Built for the factory's 40th anniversary, commissioned by Enzo Ferrari himself, this was a road-legal racecar, very reliable despite its extreme performance. The bodywork (only 101.2 lbs. – 46 kg) was built of carbon fiber, Kevlar, and honeycomb aluminum panels. There were numerous air intakes and vents (also on the rear window) for the air emitted from the crankshaft and the underbody.

The chassis practically followed the same scheme as that of the 288 GTO, with a metallic, tubular framework in keeping with the Ferrari style, with rigid, composite panels for a total weight of 257.4 lbs. (117 kg). Inside the quadrilateral suspensions were dampers that could be regulated to three positions, and an anti-roll bar. The GTO design was perfected in the engine with the V8 of almost 183.06 cu. in. (3 liters), better refrigerated and more powerful. There were four valves and two tiny Japanese turbochargers with big horizontal *intercoolers*, mechanical units that emitted great heat and due to this, availed of air intakes and vents in the chassis and even in the back window that spanned over all the mechanics. The F40 was a car designed for great performance and to this end fully responded to a driver's expectation of high, powerful performance. In track tests it hit the 202.12 mph (326 km/h) mark and took only 4.56 seconds to shoot forward from 0-62 mph (0-100 km/h) – grand results for the 1980s, supported by a powerful braking unit, which allowed for reduced stopping distance even without servo control and ABS. Efficiency performance included road holding and grip, assessable mostly on track, considering the extreme speed limits the car was capable of.

164-165 The aggressive but linear front had air flows also for the body base to enhance the grip at high speeds. The penetration coefficient was good (Cx = 0.338). The result was a track performance of 202.12 mph (326 km/h).

166-167 Air flows played an important role in the F40: the picture shows the frontal outflow vanes. Behind the doors are the air inlets for the crankshaft.

TECHNICAL SPECIFICATIONS

F40 (1987)

Engine: 90° V8 cylinders central, longitudinal

179.09 cu. in. (2,936 cc),
bores/stroke: 3.28" x 2.78" (82 x 69.5 mm)

4 valves per cylinder

Weber Marelli direct injection and two IHI turbochargers

Power: 478 hp at 7,000 rpm

longitudinal 5-speed transmission with self-lock

Tires: 245/40 ZR17" (front), 335/35 ZR17" (rear)

Wheelbase: 98" (2,450 mm)

Length: 171.6" (4,358 mm)

Width: 77.5" (1,970 mm)

Height: 44.8" (1,124 mm)

Curb-weight: 2,535 lbs. (1,150 kg)

Speed: 200.88 mph (324 km/h)

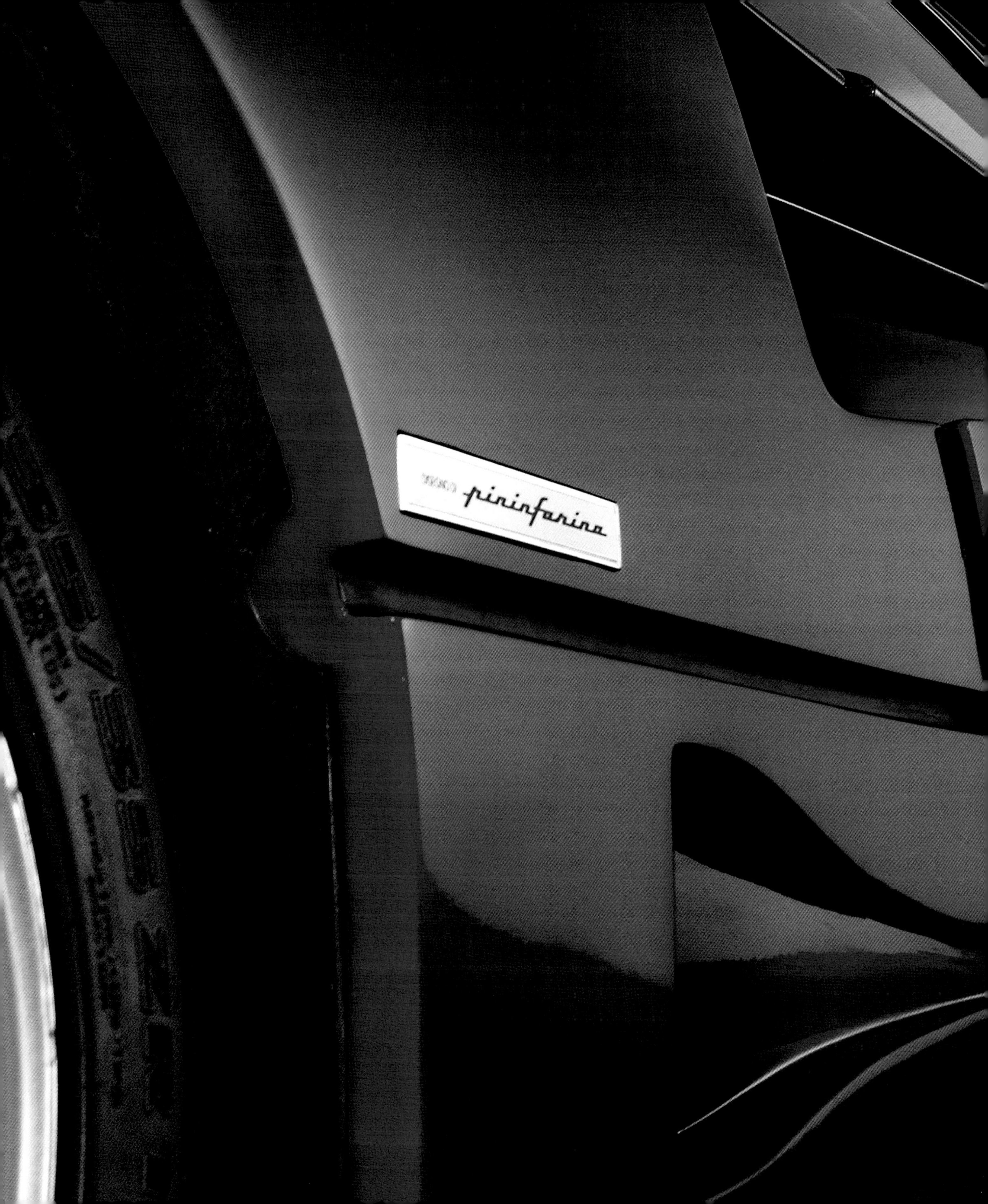
pininfarina

Ferrari 348 TB/TS

Continuous evolution

For more than a year, Enzo Ferrari (1898–1988) had no longer been at the helm of his beloved factory, which now had a new director. Everything had changed in the world of racing competitions, which dictated a new rule: the F1 turbo engines were no longer allowed. Ferrari returned to its first love, that is, the V12-cylinder engine with an absolutely new bodywork designed by John Barnard. The F40 and the Mondial T were still in production. To these the 348

TB was added, and also the evolution of the small 8 cylinders that became a 207.7 cu. in. (3,405 cc) engine, but now longitudinal with transverse gearbox and four valves per cylinder with 300 hp. The 348s remained on the market until the more evolved F355 arrived in 1994. With the new V8 there was room for the lateral radiators, now set behind the driver. The chassis, always by Pininfarina (but built by Scaglietti in steel sheets and aluminum hoods), also changed, tak-

ing up the new Ferrari styling cues such as the lateral air scoops (Testarossa type) beside the seat. The sloping nose, small grille and headlights were still of the fully integrated type. The lines were still smooth, without abrupt cuts and with an elongated roof pillar in the usual Pininfarina style. The 348 TB was shorter by an inch (2.5 cm), though with a longer wheelbase of 3.9 in. (10 cm), all for the benefit of the compartment. Alongside this Berlinetta was the 348 TS, practically a "folding

168-169 Unveiled in 1986 in the Berlinetta or open model, the 348 TB and TS (Spider) still had the longitudinal V8 and the transverse gearbox.

170-171 The tail bore the Pininfarina style lines of the "all-rear" Ferraris, with the long roof panel stiles and the wide wraparound rear window; the super-vented crankshaft was added later.

roof" version, which was very welcome, especially in the U.S.A. The "real" Spider would appear only four years later, with its canvas convertible top. With the new bodywork and greater room available, even installations and trims progressed: there was leather almost everywhere, and the imitation leather in the highly padded panels was annexed with greater care. The driver could drive more comfortably with the adjustable steering wheel, the air-conditioning was perfect in all circumstances and a complete set of analog instruments was always easy to see. However, in the new mid-engine cars, the problem of luggage room remained. Though there was no spare tire, there was little room (despite the set of Ferrari luggage), and behind the seats there was room to place some duffel bags.

Many improvements came about in technical design: the V8 was now longitudinal with transverse gearbox, engine displacement increased and output increased from 270 to 300 hp, mounted on the new load-bearing structure of the bodywork in steel, with a rear trelliswork structure holding up the engine and gearbox. The wheelbase increased by 3.9 in. (10 cm) compared to the 328 version, and the track also increased, resulting in a different type of drive. The discs were now ventilated and equipped with self-locking ABS; the steering, however, was not power-assisted. Engine displacement increased from 195.26 to 207.46 cu.

in. (3.2 to 3.4 liters) and in the bores, the position changed also – now longitudinal instead of transverse, like the gearbox which maintained the 5 speeds. These modifications, besides changing the distribution of the weight (57 percent on the rear), also transformed the drive, which became more brilliant but also more delicate, especially on wet surfaces where all that was needed was to dose the engine's accelerator and great output; its rapid response and sudden changes in trajectory, with tail swerves, could cause problems for the less expert drivers. The car could surpass 167.7 mph (270 km/h), and so it roared pleasantly (a characteristic studied by the Maranello technicians). The suspension was efficient but not very conducive to long, silent, relaxing trips. Precisely due to its very sporty features, almost race-competitive, the 348 was chosen in 1993 to inaugurate the first Ferrari Challenge, reserved for Prancing Horse clients. The foreigners were greatly impressed by this compact car and as always impressed by the endowments of the dual-faced engine: always easygoing at low speeds, transforming itself when surpassing 4,000 rpm (only half of its potential) and, beyond 5,000 rpm, spitting flames, leaving its direct rivals behind. Its performance seemed to be so exalting, so tense that in fast drives it caused apprehension in the less shrewd drivers, with very rapid transitions between the under- and oversteering that called for attention at the wheel, despite the power and efficiency of the brakes, even without the ABS.

172-173 The 348 TB/TS were produced for five years. The line takes after the Testarossa with the typical air "strakes" on the sides. Aerodynamics improved greatly with a Cx = 0.32.

174-175 In the 348 TB, the driver's seat was improved thanks to the increased wheelbase, a good 3.9 in. (10 cm) larger than that of the previous 328 GTB.

TECHNICAL SPECIFICATIONS
348 TB (1989–1994)
Engine: 90° V8 cylinders central longitudinal
207.7 cu. in. (3,405 cc), bores/stroke 3.4" x 3" (85 x 75 mm)
Bosch electronic injection
Power: 300 hp at 7,200 rpm
transversal 5-speed transmission
Tires: 215/50 ZR 17" (front), 255/50 ZR 17" (rear)
Wheelbase: 98" (2,450 mm)
Length: 169.2" (4,230 mm)
Width: 75.76" (1,894 mm)
Height: 46.8" (1,170 mm)
Curb-weight: 3,064.6 lbs. (1,393 kg)
Speed: over 170.5 mph (275 km/h)

The 1990s:

New Ideas among the GTs

THE JAPANESE WERE LAUNCHING AN ATTACK AGAINST THE WORLD OF CARS. EVEN THE PRESTIGIOUS MAKES SUCH AS

FERRARI SEEMED TO FALL UNDER THEIR BLOWS, AND YET MARANELLO HIT THE RECORD OF 4,595 UNITS PER YEAR. THEN

PRODUCTION STARTED TO DROP, AND IN 1996 THE POSTMODERN 550 MARANELLO TOOK THE STAGE. IT WAS A NEOCLAS-

SIC MARANELLO MODEL: THE 355 F1, A VERY FAST AND COMPACT V8, QUEEN OF THE MIXED SPEEDERS. FINALLY, AFTER A

SLIGHT DOWNTURN, PRODUCTION REGAINED ITS VIGOR AND IN 1995 SURPASSED 3,000 UNITS. THE SMALL 3.5-LITER 355 OF

1995 WAS BUILT, AND SO WAS ANOTHER BIG FERRARI, THE F50, A FORMULA ONE ROADSTER; IT ASTONISHED THE WORLD

AND 349 UNITS WERE BUILT. THE F50 CELEBRATED (IN ADVANCE) FERRARI'S 50TH ANNIVERSARY TOGETHER WITH THE F355

SPIDER. IN 1996, MICHAEL SCHUMACHER WON HIS FIRST TITLE, DOUBLING IT IN THE GRAND PRIX OF BELGIUM AND ITALY.

IN 1997, THE NEW WIND TUNNEL WAS INAUGURATED WHILE THE FIRST ELECTRO-ACTUATED GEAR STICKS WERE BEING

MOUNTED; THEY WOULD BE A CONSTANT IN THE FUTURE GTS. 1998 WAS CHARACTERIZED BY EXCELLENT FINANCIAL

TRENDS AND THE DEBUT OF A RENOVATED 456 M COUPE 2+2. IN 1999, HOWEVER, THE DREAM OF THE F1 PILOTS' TITLE

WAS SHATTERED DURING THE LAST MINUTES OF THE GP. AS A CONSOLATION PRIZE, FERRARI WON THE CONSTRUCTORS' TI-

TLE AFTER 16 YEARS. THE OVERWHELMING VICTORIES IN FORMULA ONE WOULD FINALLY COME IN 2000.

Ferrari 456 GT

Smaller but more roomy

TECHNICAL SPECIFICATIONS
456 GT (1992–2004)

Engine: 65° V12 cylinders

333.91 cu. in. (5,474 cc),
bores/stroke: 3.52" x 3" (88 x 75 mm)

Bosch electronic injection

Power: 442 hp at 6,250 rpm

automatic 6-speed transmission
with 3 ratios on the rear axle

Tires: 255/45 ZR 17" (front), 285/40 ZR 17" (rear)

Length: 189.2" (4,730 mm)

Width: 76.8" (1,920 mm)

Height: 52" (1,300 mm)

Curb-weight: 3,718 lbs. (1,690 kg)

Speed: 191.89 mph (309.5 km/h)

Formula One had been disappointing, above all because the revolutionary F92 A, fantastic on paper, in fact proved to be almost a disaster for Jean Alesi and Ivan Capelli, who were not able to compete with the leaders in the Grand Prix. Big changes in production came about (4,833 cars, with 2,419 employees), whereas this "elderly" 365 GT4 2+2 of 1972 became a 400 GT series in 1976. Ferrari had pursued a constant development line, retaining its rather square chassis that remained in vogue up to the arrival of this 456 GT in 1992. Destined in turn to remain in production for more than a decade, it offered the best of the Ferrari design and four years later would be flanked by the automatic version. A true and proper leap in style came about, passing from the squared and slightly aloof look to the more modern and curvaceous lines of the 412, which would be maintained

also in Maranello's succeeding four-seater version. Engineer Lorenzo Ramaciotti, who designed it, declared that he was satisfied with his work: "Still today, the 456 to my mind was quite a success. Perhaps I could have moved the wheels forward by about 5.85 in. (15 cm) because the wheelbase was too short. In 12 years, however, we did not change much." The 456 was astounding, and inasmuch as it was shorter by 3.12 in. (8 cm) and its wheelbase shorter by a good 3.9 in. (10 cm); it was, however, wider by 5.07 in. (13 cm) and conformed to the new laws of aerodynamics with numberless air louvers on the nose. What was striking above all was the broader crankshaft on the side, which became also an important stylistic motif. The new chassis was more coherent with the aerodynamics of those years (good coefficient of $Cx = 0.336$). Also clearly successful were the air vents at the tail, with mini flaps that kept the rear axle

more stable at high speeds, together with one of the first faired-in underbodies to contribute to the car's grip. The bodywork was very lightweight, with door and roof panel in steel, in pursuit of limited weight: 3,718 lbs. (1,690 kg) instead of the 4,147 lbs. (1,885 kg) of the preceding 412 model. Effort was made to distribute the masses in the best way (51 percent in front and 49 percent at the rear), to facilitate handling, stability and passenger comfort. Also, the suspensions were decisive, with three rigidity modes (Soft, Medium, Sport). Everything in the 456 was finalized to ensure the utmost comfort possible with modern technology and Italian handcraft skills. The result was a 2+2 coupe suitable for long, comfortable and fast traveling (recorded at 192.2 mph – 310 km/h), very livable, with seats at their best, finishing in Connolly leather and imitation leather to make the compartment cozier than

ever. Big and small amenities could be enjoyed, such as air-conditioning, radio, instruments, adjustments and commands always at hand, and when needed, up to 442 hp. By then safety was obligatory, so the car was equipped with ABS, safety bars in the doors and two airbags; however, the anti-skid and anti-sideslip devices were missing. The trunk was astonishing with 19,282.32 cu. in. (316 liters) capacity, exploitable to the utmost with a precise set of suitcases (lovely and expensive). It was a top car that satisfied even the more demanding clients, given that it remained on the price list for years, while the trends (and cars) changed so often.

It traveled at high levels with the so-called transaxle scheme (front engine, gearbox at the rear), the four-cam V12 cylinders and Bosch indirect injection. The uncommon engine in light alloy weighed 517 lbs. (235 kg), with four overhead camshafts, toothed

belts, four valves per cylinder with a great output of 442 hp (it was after all, a Ferrari) and a very high engine torque, ensuring great elasticity on the road. It had an IX6-speed automatic transmission with three on the rear axle and self-locking differential, to better distribute the power onto the rear wheels. It was all based on a new tubular chassis, with quadrilateral suspension and electrically controlled (independent) suspension (with three different settings and command station). On the road the massive 456, despite its weight of 3,718 lbs. (1,690 kg), was not disappointing: it hit the 192.2 mph (310 km/h) mark, sprang forward in the right manner, kept the trajectories correctly with a limited roll and a constant grip on curves, and always responded well to the driver. It was definitely a very classy coupe, and with its engine and behavior really proved to be a guarantee of comfortable and safe traveling.

178-179 The 456 of 1992 paved a new path for Ferrari design of that decade. With the line always by Pininfarina, transaxle mechanics was the modern version of the Ferrari 275 GTB of the 1970s.

180-181 The 456 had a precise setting, slightly traditional but very balanced for a four-seater sports car. The line remained practically unchanged up to 2004, when the 612 Scaglietti arrived.

Ferrari F355

A good Italian design

There were signs of the Ferrari picking up again in Formula One, although the newborn 412 T1 (for Jean Alesi and Gerhard Berger) was still unable to steer the Ferrari to the top. Production was going full blast: the factories furnished 2,639 cars, among which the F355, with its tiny 8-cylinder engine, marked a turning point when Maranello passed from the management of engineer Piero Fusaro to that of Luca Cordero di Montezemolo. The F355 seemed to be a normal evolution of the 348, but in reality was totally new: a silent evolution which, however, left its mark. As usual, its name had to be interpreted: "35" stood for the engine displacement (about 213.5 cu. in. – 3500 cc), whereas the last "5" indicated the novelty of valves per cylinder. The F355 was undoubtedly a Ferrari and one could see this by the classic, small grille, drooping hood with fully integrated lights, air intakes on the sides and roof panel with the long rear stiles which almost reached the tail, delimiting the space reserved for the engine. Its dimensions were practically those of its predecessor, the 348 (length:

13.95 ft. – 4.25 m); width: 6.23 ft. (1.9 m); height: 3.93 ft. (1.2 m). A year later, also for the F355, the total Spider stepped in, though without the grille, placed alongside the 355 GTS with a convertible top.

It was the first Ferrari to have Formula One solutions, such as the five valves per cylinder (three for suction, two for exhaust), and also had a progressive transmission. With Pininfarina design and Scaglietti steel construction, the utterly sporty F355 was also more comfortable: once the driver squeezed into the compartment, he could enjoy an ideally sporty space. What was not visible was the evolution of studies on the flat base, decisive in Formula One. Parts of the preceding 348 GTB, such as the hood and the front fenders, were retained, taking up the motif of the air intakes on the sides for the lateral radiators. A set of various materials gave rise to details for a sports car with an undoubtedly Ferrari personality, with its constant urge to achieve excellent profiling and aerodynamic load, to be able to overtake rivals by exploiting the self-regulating suspension.

182-183 The F355 Spider of 1995 was an open but also very elegant sports car, and a constant in the Maranello compact models. It delivered 380 hp, with adjustable suspension and a top speed of 182.9 mph (295 km/h).

184-185 The sportive talents of the F355 are exalted in the Berlinetta of 1994, a totally new model with its longitudinal V8 engine of 213.57 cu. in. (3.5 liters) with transversal 6-speed gears and servo steering.

"Ground leveled," fast and safe driving

As in the 348, the driver's seat was low as possible in a cabin that offered the best for mid-engine sports cars, where the materials were first-class: Connolly leather, imitation leather, fitted carpeting and plastic. The various commands were correctly positioned, setting up a car that was functional and pleasing for touring, but also for speed driving, with conventional, analog instruments integrated, and various indicator lights. The Ferrari not only manufactured racecars, but increasingly offered that mix of technology and design that was remarkable also in the compartment: the analogic instruments were well in view (but a lot depended on the adjustable steering wheel), and besides the very sporty perforated pedal there was a central console with the renowned sector grid of the 6-speed paddle gearshift. There were also various buttons for air-conditioning and the adjustable mirrors. The spare tire was missing, replaced by an emergency fire extinguisher, and in front the compartment was big enough for a pair of suitcases (the bench behind the seats could also be used). If the mechanics took up the very upgraded scheme of the 348, aerodynamics took a step forward to exploit the air flows for better balance between the down forces that maintained road grip and the profiling that increased speed and saved on fuel. The front louvers directed the outgoing air flux to the base of the body, at the height of the gear, whereas the shape of the vertical loads on the chassis contributed to its shape. Specific research on aerodynamics seemed to be one of the key elements behind the F355's road performance. It was a very fast Berlinetta that hit the 182.9 mph (295 km/h) mark (clocked) and accelerat-

186-187 The F355 was the first Ferrari Spider to be produced in steel and aluminum with the electrical convertible top. The photo shows the air inlets on the sides for the V8 engine and the rear discs.

ed from 0 to 62 mph (0 to 100 km/h) in 7.4 seconds. With a V8 of 380 hp structure, sports driving was greatly satisfying, but it was not advisable to give in to too much enthusiasm seeing that the power output was always at hand, though the electronic safety measures (ABS, anti-skid, ASR) were always there for a prompt intervention. The driving was ever more precise and fast, and also eliminated the overly rapid and sudden reactions of the 348 which, when all was said and done, made use of the same mechanics. Such upgrades would be appreciated even more on the 1999 F360 Modena.

TECHNICAL SPECIFICATIONS
355 GTB (1994–1999)
Engine: 90° V8 cylinders central longitudinal
213.25 cu. in. (3,496 cc),
bores/stroke: 3.4" x 3.08" (85 x 77 mm)
Bosch electronic injection
Power: 380 hp at 8,250 rpm
6-speed transversal transmission
Tires: 225/40 ZR 18" (front), 265/40 ZR 18" (rear)
Wheelbase: 98" (2,450 mm)
Curb-weight: 2,970 lbs. (1,350 kg)
Length: 170" (4,250 mm)
Width: 76" (1,900 mm)
Height: 46.8" (1,170 mm)
Speed: 182.88 mph (294.97 km/h)

Ferrari 512 M

The last giant

TECHNICAL SPECIFICATIONS
512 M (1994–1996)

Engine: 180° V12 cylinders central
301.52 cu. in. (4,943 cc),
bores/stroke: 32.8" x 31.2" (82 x 78 mm)
4 overhead camshafts with toothed belt
4 valves per cylinder
Power: 440 hp at 6,750 rpm
5-speed transmission
Tires: 235/40 ZR 18" (front), 295/35 ZR 18" (rear)
4 ventilated disc brakes
Wheelbase: 102" (2,550 mm)
Length: 179.2" (4,480 mm)
Width: 79.04" (1,976 mm)
Height: 45.4" (1,135 mm)
Curb-weight: 3,201 lbs. (1,455 kg)
Speed: 195.3 mph (315 km/h)

In the 1990s, something changed in the world of the very fast, sportiest sports cars, those which could have sped (on track) at 186 mph (300 km/h). But drivers, too, had changed; they had obligations and limits to respect but wanted to drive fast and comfortably without having to work too hard. Ferrari, before any other automaker, took note of the problems that were creating turmoil in those particular times, and started to slowly transform itself: it produced over 2,600 cars yearly, but had to cater to its most demanding and faithful clients with new and attractive models. The 512 M was the last representative of a "breed," which by then seemed to be declining, and prepared to be replaced by models with a different outlook, though deeply rooted in the past. It was the heir of the 365 GT4 BB family, produced in the 1970s but still in vogue with its exclusive, unique

Boxer engine and 12 cylinders in two opposite banks which, after over 20 years, had reached the maximum development sustained by modern electronics. The Boxer engine of 301.52 cu. in. (4,943 cc), weighing 493.9 lbs. (224.5 kg), had four valves per cylinder and fuel injection, delivered 440 hp, and also ensured a hefty engine torque, useful even in normal driving. This was a two-seater Berlinetta designed by Pininfarina and built by Scaglietti all in aluminum, in conformance to the old style, but with slightly sharper lines that were, however, easily recognizable. It was 14.8 ft. (4.5 m) long, almost 6.6 ft. (2 m) wide and 3.72 ft. (1.135 m) high, with its front moved forward and still very low, with lateral radiators (as in the Testarossa). The lines became more curvaceous, similar to that of the Sport Prototype racecar, with some style-lines that have forever remained in the chronicles of car design,

such as the roof panel stiles extended up to the tail and the lateral air louvers (which the English nicknamed "cheese graters"). The 20-year-old pop-up lights were eliminated; the front now possessed a bolder personality with a classic Ferrari grille (fake, only for air-conditioning) and glass-covered lights. With the new front structure, the front compartment of 15,255 cu. in. (250 liters) also became available for luggage. Other features: included the new helical gear wheels (dismountable) for the great 18-inch tires, and increasingly precise research on aerodynamics, also at the underbody. The refined interior boasted seats in Connolly leather, well upholstered and profiled, comfortable and adjustable, even if many preferred to adopt (on request) the racer type of seats with body in composite materials conceived for extreme super-sports purposes. The analog in-

struments were arranged on two dashboards, one in front of the driver and a smaller one in the sub-bridge. At the console, the central tunnel had all the service buttons (from air-conditioning to the lights and the adjustable seats), dominated by the gearstick inserted in the classic sector grid. The driver was in the best driving conditions since, besides electrically adjusted seats, he could also adjust the steering wheel to favor his "work." The entire compartment had a classy finish in Connolly leather. The air-conditioning was fast and efficient, considering the class of the 512 M and the great amount of heat the engine emitted behind the driver.

Just one look could tell you that this was not a car for everyone. On the other hand, when approaching its redline, needless to say, you had to be very careful and particularly gentle given its output and weight,

3,201 lbs. (1,455 kg), which made it behave very roughly when pushed more than necessary, since drive control electronics was still being developed. But the 512 M, considered the last representative of a not-too-current technology, would have been missed so much by the most passionate Ferrari faithful due to its fascination and the brutality of its performance, and because it was the fruit of technology beyond compare, and had carried over the Formula One and Sport Prototype technology. Even today, it is considered a collector's item and museum piece and is also highly valued in auctions. Some Ferrari cars of this model were transformed into Spiders by Pininfarina and by the Milanese, Pavesi. But as the head of the 512 M line declared: "It has remained as an icon of the 1990s when it was impossible to undertake any substantial restyling without upsetting its original spirit."

188-189 The extreme and last evolution of the Testarossa of 1984. With Pininfarina design and built by Scaglietti, it had an aluminum chassis with steel doors and roof panel. Its 305.1-cu. in. (5-liter) Boxer engine delivered 440 hp but the car still weighed 3,201 lbs. (1,455 kg). Its production still held for another 10 years until the arrival of the 550 Maranello.

190-191 The 512 M had an exclusive style, highlighted by the streaks on its sides for the air inlets for the rear radiators and the Boxer engine. It made a noteworthy leap forward (43.1 in. – 1,095 mm) and the car's profiling benefitted from a Cx of 0.36 and a top speed of 195.3 mph (315 km/h).

Ferrari F50

From another planet

May 1995: this newly designed Ferrari supercar seemed to come from outer space, as if it were a Formula One that had to circulate on the road. It was capable of sensational performance, backed by the forever extraordinary V12 of 286 cu. in. (4.7 liters) delivering 520 hp. After a good four years of design in search of the best formula, it was produced in a limited series for collectors (350). Its chassis was in ultralight carbon fiber, weighing 225 lbs. (102 kg), but extremely rigid with a bodywork also in carbon. The car was a Spider-Berlinetta, which to the most critical Ferrari faithful did not seem like a beauty queen but was certainly functional. It was a diligent study in aerodynamics for the extreme performance announced, with "push rod" suspensions (push-arm) also deriving from the F1, but it was able to adapt itself perfectly to normal roads as well as the tracks for which it was destined. Its line was really striking even if many did not really consider it a beauty, and was the fruit of long and painstaking studies on Pininfarina aerodynamics. This was a compact coupe Spider (about 14.8 in or 4.5 m), with considerable aerodynamic loads (682 lbs. – 310 kg) especially at the tail (65 percent), to achieve greater stability at maximum speeds (192 mph – 310 km/h). The line provided for an advanced driver position almost on the front axle, large rear with a big fixed flap that loaded the rear axle, and enhanced easy steering. Even the air flows in the underbody were used to ensure greater grip when speeding. Its chassis had an illustrious forerunner, the Mythos, the 1989 "dream car" by Pininfarina. Garish elements and F50 features were the two "hunches" at the rear, above the roll bars. The body evidenced aerodynamic research with a good Cx (profiling) of 0.36, but with a significant downforce coefficient to ensure grip at high speeds. All these were enriched by air inlets on the front and sides to exploit the air flux countering the car. Not all were perfect solutions, but they satisfied precise aerodynamic needs and the result of studies that were not only an end in themselves; they were useful also to the succeeding Ferrari-Pininfarina cars.

TECHNICAL SPECIFICATIONS
F50 BERLINETTA-SPIDER (1995)

Engine: 65° V12 cylinders central
286.57 cu. in. (4,698 cc),
bores/stroke: 3.4 x 2.8" (85 x 69 mm)
4 overhead camshafts
5 valves per cylinder
Power: 520 hp at 8,500 rpm
6-speed transmission
Tires: 245/35 ZR 18" (front),
335/30 ZR18" (rear)
4 ventilated discs
Wheelbase: 101.6" (2580 mm)
Length: 177" (4,480 mm)
Width: 78.2" (1,986 mm)
Height: 44.1" (1,120 mm)
Curb-weight: 2,706 lbs. (1,230 kg)
Speed: 202 mph (325 km/h)

192-193 The F50, a gem designed
to celebrate the Maranello company's
50th anniversary, was an extreme rear-
engine Berlinetta with 12 cylinders and
astounding performance, 520 hp and
201.5 mph (325 km/h).

194-195 The nose also highlights the result of
research on air flows with dynamic inlets for
radiators and brakes with the related air vents.
This Berlinetta racecar, almost an F1 with 12
cylinders, was even good for road traffic but
had a limited production (349 units).

Nothing superfluous: this is a Ferrari

To be able to save on weight, the very expensive F50s had nothing more than what was indispensable for "Ferrari-style" driving. In the compartment carved out in the bodywork structure, the finishing was minimal with rubber mats, Connolly leather and a special breathable canvas on the seats (available in two sizes). An essential dashboard and a counter with the analog instruments (speedometer and rev counter) integrated with the digital ones for con-sumption (fuel and oil). The dashboard, in conformance with the house rules, took after those of the F1 and was controlled by microprocessors, all inserted in the apparently simple but very functional dashboard, a mix of leather and carbon. The steering wheel was fixed but each driver found his ideal position by shifting the chair as preferred. The controls most used were the lever-commands on the column.

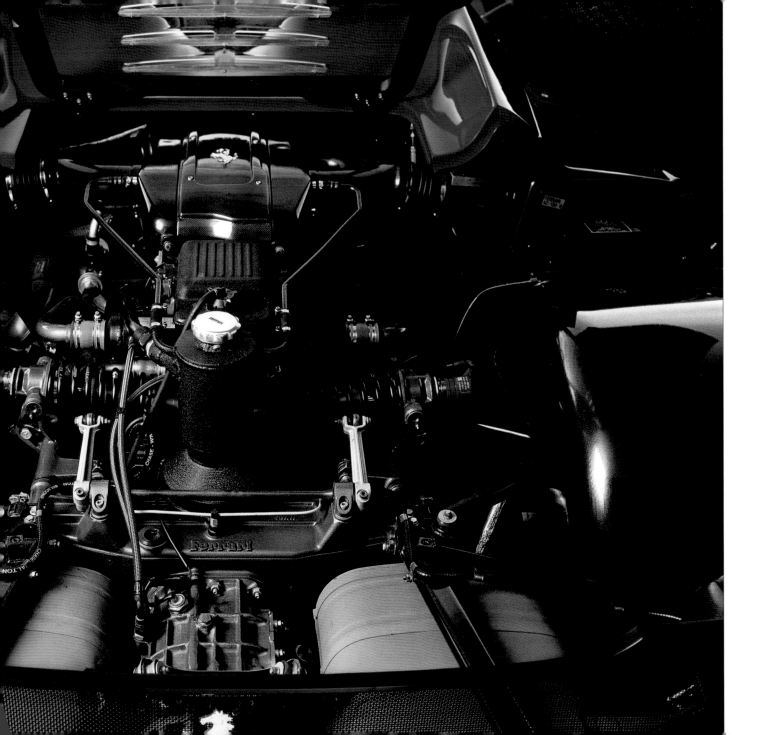

Taking on
a Schumacher air

In short, the car was practically a Formula One car in terms of body preparation, with a central body in carbon fiber weighing 204 lbs. (102 kg), which was more than double that of a single-seater of the 1990s, plus the various metallic components like the suspension, radiators, fans and roll bars. The overall weight was just 2,706 lbs. (1,230 kg), in-

cluding the V12 engine built like the F1 of those times, in spheroidal cast iron, whereas the heads were of aluminum with four overhead camshafts. Also the suspension system was the race type with quadrilateral arms and dampers with sensors that sent signals to a control unit. Though there were many electronic controls, the drive appeared to be

very inviting for drivers in search of Formula One sensations and 520 hp, relatively easy) to tame and handle sensibly even during daily trips. It was a car not only for collectors but also for ardent enthusiasts. All the other fundamental components (brakes without ABS, steering without the servo mechanism) were perfect for any situation, with a behavioral precision that was ideal for those times. Even the aspect of comfort, for a car "philosophically" designed for racing, was more than acceptable. These were all very useful indicators for the upcoming Ferraris. And Maranello would keep on producing such extreme fireballs, as proven by the Enzo model in 2002.

Ferrari 550 Maranello

Return to the future

TECHNICAL SPECIFICATIONS

550 MARANELLO (1996–2002)

Engine: 65° V 12 cylinders

333.91 cu. in. (5,474 cc),
bores/stroke: 3.52" x 3" (88 x 75 mm)

4 valves per cylinder

Bosch electronic injection

Power: 485 hp at 7,000 rpm

6-speed transmission on the rear axle

Tires: 255/40 ZR 18" (front), 295/35 ZR 18" (rear)

Curb-weight: 2,420 lbs. (1,100 kg)

Length: 182" (4,550 mm)

Width: 77.4" (1,935 mm)

Height: 51.08" (1,277 mm)

Weight: 3,718 lbs. (1,690 kg)

Speed: 198.4 mph (320) km/h

Winds of novelty were blowing over Maranello in Formula One, where the new arrival, twice world champion Michael Schumacher, seemed ready to conquer that World Championship which had been so elusive since 1979. There were surprises also in production (3,363 cars) and the BB Berlinetta, queen since 1972, gave up its position to the more traditional 550 Maranello, with the number indicating displacement of the now anterior V12 engine. The car took up some solutions of the coupe of the 1960s: engine in front, transaxle gears and suspensions on independent wheels. Substantially, it seemed to take inspiration from the unforgettable Daytona of 1968. Of course after almost 30 years, many things had matured: electronics had come on the scene, aerodynamics had evolved and suspensions were now suitable also in view of the new dictates of the market, where staggering performance alone no longer sufficed. Apart from such extreme outputs (485 hp), its characteristics did not scare drivers any more since the electronic "services" (ABS, anti-skids, etc.) eliminated most of the problems involved in sporty driving. The Maranello (with a good aerodynamic coefficient Cx = 0.33, thanks to 5,000 hours of wind tunnel tests) was a Berlinetta that surpassed 197.16 mph (318 km/h) and was also comfortable for long trips, equipped with the refined items available on the supercar market. In the new Pininfarina trend, style lines of the past re-emerged, such as the clipped tail and the tendency to move the compact compartment backward, with livability for two people and a bench for items other than luggage. It was a stylistically pleasant coupe that all the Ferrari fans liked; precisely due to these features, it would remain in production for six years, to be replaced by the next 575

M Maranello – one of its upgraded clones, overhauled in all aspects. The entire compartment setting was decisively classic, but seen in light of the new trends, it was still one that adapted itself to the needs of sports driving of the 1990s, allowing a better layout of the analog instruments in the two complementary dashboards in front of the driver. Almost all the controls appeared on the central console, and the seats were built with care to suit every type of driver: it had eight adjusting levels, and, on request, the race types could be mounted. Everything suited with the class of the car, its two front airbags and automatic air-conditioning system. The luggage trunk was a bit small (11,288.7 cu. in. – 185 liters), but integrated with the space behind the seats. Also the finishing, Connolly leather and generous upholstery all over, satisfied the demanding Ferrari clients who could avail themselves of ergonomically arranged controls they could activate without problems, even while driving.

In the Ferrari super sports cars, there was a return to classic schemes, overhauled in light of new theories. So once again the transaxle schemes were in vogue with transmission (6-speed) on the rear axle, whereas the anterior, V12 of aluminum, had four valves per cylinder, suction conduits and exhaust pipes that were geometrically variable, taking after those of the F1. The bodywork returned to a tubular structure stiffened by metallic panels that enhanced silence, comfort and drivability, and an independent suspension with gas-regulating dampers on two levels. To improve the grip and handling, the anterior track was increased to 1.79 in. (4.6 cm). Also the steering was electronically controlled. With such exclusive quality mechanics and electronics considered flawless for the 1990s, the Maranello was unbeatable in long trips thanks to the V12, very powerful and always spruced up from 1,500 revs in sixth gear up to over 8,000, assisted by an ever perfect drive even when correcting small errors. The gearbox was the upgraded type with the sector grid: time would have to pass before paddles appeared on the steering wheel. For those who are keen on pure performance, the Maranello model reached and surpassed 197.16 mph (318 km/h), accelerating from 0 to 62 mph (100 km/h) in 5.1 seconds. In those times no other sports car was able to keep up with this model. Such performance was also confirmed by the Maranello cars, which took part in sports competitions worldwide. The standard version in 1998, for example, on an oval track in Ohio, established a world record, speeding constantly at 186 mph (300 km/h).

202-203 The classic 550 remained in production for four years and in 2006 was replaced by the 599 GTB, which conserved the setting of its mechanics.

204-205 The slim profile of the 575 M practically retained that of the 550 with the same aerodynamic coefficient (Cx = 0.335) and the same setting as to mechanics.

Ferrari 360 Modena

206-207 *Built in 1999, the 360 Modena carried on along the lines of the previous F355 but was lighter by 220 lbs. (100 kg) than the preceding Spider due to ample use of aluminum. It had 400 hp and a longitudinal engine-gearbox (also electro-actuated).*

208-209 *The 360 possessed a harmonic and streamlined style. Thanks to its flat underbody and its better profiled chassis (Cx = 0.35), the car had a better grip also at 180 mph (290 km/h).*

Light and sculptured by the wind

1999 started well for Ferrari: it had the best Formula One car (the F399) and the best driver (Michael Schumacher), though in reality it managed to win just the Constructors' title. Production was doing better now at 3,699 cars yearly. The new 360 Modena had arrived: the number now indicated the engine displacement of about 219.6 cu. in. (3,600 cc), the latest evolution of the compact "all rear" conception. This car was uncommon in terms of mechanics, aerodynamics and the use of materials, especially aluminum. It was, of course, more evolved than its predecessor, the F355, and was 14.68 ft. (4.477 m) long, 8.85 in. (22.7 cm) more, with a wheelbase of 8.52 ft. (2.60 m) (greater by 5.85 in. – 15 cm), and was also much lighter (132 lbs. – 60 kg less). This was not just a mere

restyling; it really perfected each component. The classical Ferrari grille disappeared, having been replaced by two almost lateral air inlets for the radiators, which moved back to the front, also to improve the weight distribution. Another aesthetic motif was destined to appear also on the succeeding Ferraris. Through the great rear window one could discern the V8 engine, upgraded in displacement (from 213.19 to 218.74 cu. in. (3,495 to 3,586 cc) and in output (400 hp, 20 more). Another fundamental novelty was the more extensive use of aluminum, not only in the bodywork but also in mechanics: engine, chassis and suspensions were now in this metal, and saved 132 lbs., (60 kg) ensuring also a greater rigidity that resulted in more precision in the handling and stability. Each formal solu-

tion was studied to serve aerodynamic demands as well. In the front where the grille once was, there was now a deviator that directed the air flows to the underbody to obtain the desired ground effect, improving the grip at high speeds. At the sides, the two big air inlets and grid disappeared leaving room for two smaller ones, almost at the bottom, and another two on the rear fenders, at the base of the stiles. These were designed to air out the engine shaft without interrupting the profile of the side and improve the air flow up to the rear mini-*spoilers*, which, together with the deflector, enhanced the underbody air flow. And then in 2000 the "total" Spider appeared (that is, without the grille), heavier by 132 lbs. (60 kg) due to the necessary reinforcements to the structure.

TECHNICAL SPECIFICATIONS

360 MODENA (1999–2004)

Engine: 90° V8 cylinders central longitudinal
218.74 cu. in. (3,586 cc),
bores/stroke: 3.4" x 3.16" (85 x 79 mm)

Bosch electronic injection

Power: 400 hp at 8,500 rpm

longitudinal, also progressive 6-speed transmission

Tires: 215/45 ZR 18" (front), 275/40 ZR 18" (rear)

Wheelbase: 104" (2,600 mm)

Curb-weight: 2,838 lbs. (1,290 kg)

Length: 176.2" (4,477 mm)

Width: 76.92" (1,923 mm)

Height: 48.56" (1,214 mm)

Speed: 184.63 mph (297.8 km/h)

210-211 and 212-213 The 360 Spider came on the scene in 2000, and bore the same mechanics as the Berlinetta but was heavier because of the necessarily reinforced structure. With air inlets for the crankshaft, fuel injection and radiator, it was an improvement in all ways thanks to the greater attention paid to aerodynamics. Its V8 engine of 0.936 cu. in. (3.6 liters) delivered 400 hp with the 6-speed gearbox, which was longitudinal and electro-actuated. It had an "automatic" convertible top.

In the Ferrari models of this type, what was most desired was a driver's seat similar to that of the race-cars but without forgoing greater livability onboard. This was made possible in the 360 due to greater room (with the elongated wheelbase) and a more accurate interior design. The driver, above all, benefitted from this, and had almost everything at hand, not having to lose time finding the controls arranged all over the dashboard or on the narrow central console. Also the instrumentation, almost all in analog form with a few digital items, was easily readable, though scat-

tered all over the dashboard. The seats were well made, well profiled and always upholstered with excellent Connolly leather, giving the best support to the driver who could drive in a relaxed manner, also thanks to the 6-speed gearshift with paddle commands (very fast) on the steering column – a pleasure very difficult to forgo. Fast and efficient air-conditioning and a better rear view were the other benefits found when seated at the steering wheel. The car also featured a sufficiently large front trunk, 10,983.6 cu. in. (180 liters) capacity, plus another 4,271 cu. in. (70 liters) in the space behind the seats.

Technology and polished drive

As earlier said, the most significant variant was certainly the extensive use of aluminum, which now involved, besides the bodywork, the entire chassis, with a central roof panel and two tubular subpanels in front of and behind the engine and suspension (also in aluminum and adjustable in two configurations, for normal and sports driving). Aerodynamics was so vital for such fast sports cars. The profiling was very good (Cx = 0.33) but became fundamental for the grip, ensured by a good loading of the bodywork and by the ground effect. On the 360, at maximum speed a dynamic load of 396 lbs. (180 kg) was uniformly distributed. The engine, almost unchanged, ex-

ploited the slight increase of engine displacement (only 5.55 cu. in. – 91 cc) and new fluid dynamics (collectors with variable geometrics), that produced greater output (400 hp instead of 380) but above all greater usability in all conditions. Safety was adequate for the time since, besides the ABS, the car possessed two anti-skids for driving mode options (normal or sports). Road handling also improved compared to the 355: despite the increase in output, the 360 was less frisky in its reactions and guaranteed enhanced "sporting" comfort during long trips. It was a good starting point for its 2004 successor, the F430.

The 2000s:

The Era of Supercars

A NEW FERRARI "RED" ERA HAD BEGUN; SCHUMACHER FINALLY WON THE WORLD TITLE FOR THE PRANCING HORSE. EVEN THE ECONOMIC SITUATION WAS DECISIVELY POSITIVE: THE YEAR HAD CLOSED WITH HIGHLY INCREASED PROFITS WHILE PRODUCTION SURPASSED 4,000 UNITS WITH NEW SPIDERS, AMONG WHICH WAS THE 550 BARCHETTA. SALES WERE BOOMING WITH STRONG UPTRENDS ON THE HISTORICAL MARKETS. ANOTHER F1 ROAD CAR WAS BUILT TO CELEBRATE THE FORMULA ONE VICTORIES: THE FABULOUS ENZO WHICH, WITH THE 660 HP OF ITS 12-CYLINDER ENGINE AND ELECTRO-AC-TUATED GEARBOX, WAS MARANELLO'S MOST POWERFUL GT. TURNOVERS INCREASED AND SO DID PRODUCTION (4,236 UNITS) WITH THE ARRIVAL OF THE COMPACT 360 GT FOR THE RACES AND THE 575 M MARANELLO. 2004 BROUGHT AN-OTHER FORMULA ONE VICTORY FOR SCHUMACHER AND THE FERRARI – THE SEVENTH WORLD TITLE FOR THE GERMAN DRIV-ER. THE 612 SCAGLIETTI WAS UNVEILED AS THE SUCCESSOR OF THE 575 M, THE FIRST 12-CYLINDER WITH ELECTRO-ACTU-ATED GEAR LEVERS. AFTER THE VICTORIES OF 2004, SCHUMACHER AND FERRARI FOUND IT DIFFICULT TO REPEAT THE TRI-UMPHANT PERFORMANCES, SINCE IN 2005 BOTH FELT THE WEIGHT OF THEIR COMPETITORS. THE U.S. MARKET WAS NOT TO BE IGNORED AS IT HAD ALWAYS BEEN A GREAT RESERVOIR FOR SALES. SO IN 2005, FERRARI BUILT A LIMITED NUMBER (559 UNITS) OF THE SUPERAMERICA SPIDER, WITH AN ORIGINAL CONVERTIBLE GLASS TOP; ITS V12 ENGINE OF 350.62 CU. IN. (5,748 CC) AND 540 HP HIT THE TOP SPEED OF 198.4 MPH (320 KM/H). THERE WAS ALSO THE FXX, THE ENZO RACE CAR (29 UNITS) WITH 800 HP AND 213.9 MPH (345 KM/H). 2006 COULD HAVE BEEN ANOTHER "SCHUMACHER YEAR" BUT UN-FORESEEN EVENTS DEPRIVED HIM OF THE EIGHTH WORLD TITLE. INSTEAD, BRILLIANT RESULTS WERE SEEN IN PRODUCTION WITH THE F430, 612 AND 599 GTB, RESULTING IN 5,671 CARS YEARLY (121 IN CHINA). 2007 WAS THE YEAR OF KIMI RÄIKKÖ-NEN AND HIS F2007, AND HE WON THE DRIVERS' WORLD TITLE – THE LAST FOR THAT DECADE. IN THE MEANTIME, 6,000 MORE CARS WERE PRODUCED.

Ferrari 550 Barchetta Pininfarina

The world's fastest

TECHNICAL SPECIFICATIONS
550 BARCHETTA PININFARINA (2000)

Engine: 65° V12 cylinders

333.91 cu. in. (5,474 cc),
bores/stroke: 3.52" x 3" (88 x 75 mm)

4 valves per cylinder

Bosch electronic injection

Power: 485 hp at 7,000 rpm

rear axle 6-speed transmission

Tires: 255/40 ZR 18" (front), 295/35 ZR 18" (rear)

Length: 182" (4,550 mm)

Width: 77.4" (1,935 mm)

Height: 51.08" (1,277 mm)

Weight: 3,718 lbs. (1,690 kg)

Speed: 186 mph (300 km/h)

It was not surprising that all manufacturers tried to revise the models that were crucial to the growth of their trademarks, to boost their prestige and of course, sell more cars. In the case of Ferrari, the link with the past was stronger than ever, because the 1948 Barchetta had been Maranello's first model to gain worldwide fame for its sports victories and for its two-seater total Spider line. At its debut in 1949, it won the Mille Miglia and a fervid young man, Gianni Agnelli, had one built for himself, with a particular color (blue/green, with the interior in cream-tone leather). This Barchetta of the year 2000, then considered the fastest in the world, was also coveted by Luca Cordero di Montezemolo, Ferrari's president, who unveiled it that year, underscoring the fact that it was supposed to be used only as an open Spider. With just a preset limited production (448) according to a policy which was not new to Maranello, it used various materials: steel for the doors, aluminum for the hoods and front fenders, and fiberglass for the bumper shields. Pininfarina was assigned the task of giving it the best finishing with old and new stylistic motifs – a successful undertaking, given that all the cars were quickly sold. The starting point was the Berlinetta 550 of 1996, which was supposed to suggest, or rather impose, the Ferrari's style-lines also on this exclusive total Spider which, as the designers foresaw, had to go down in history like all the cars of the 1950s. Engineer Ramaciotti of Pininfarina, head of the Barchetta design, said: "We practically re-

designed a great part of the Spider which could not have been just a simple Spider 550 without its roof panel: besides the windshield we also restructured the compartment and the entire central-rear portion of the Berlinetta, renouncing the use of the coupe Spider's renowned technology with metallic modular top."

The Barchetta did have an emergency canvas top. But after use, it had to be folded and packed into its specific bag in the trunk. With such a rear drive and after the new and smaller windshield, even the chassis was redesigned with soft but firm lines, new volumes and a short clipped tail which gave even more impetus to the front, in line with a typical setting of the past, another style-line to stress the presence of the powerful 12 cylinders of 335.61 cu. in. (5.5 liters) with 485 hp and more or less the same bulk as the 550 Maranello, with a weight equivalent to 3,718 lbs. (1,690 kg) – despite the stiffening needed to maintain the same dynamic characteristics of the Berlinetta. In 2001 all the prototypes estimated were delivered to the clients. The apparently competitive spirit of this custom-built car also needed a special interior design, with a drive shifted towards the rear axle to confirm the car's peculiar spirit, numerous carbon fiber inserts, and few essential controls for a drive virtually taking inspiration from that of the past. But it had all the necessary components of a 2000 sports car, with adjustable steering wheel in height and tilt, and the two airbags or the small windshield in high-resistance tubular steel, more slanted compared to the Berlinetta. In the entire compartment upholstered with a special fabric, the Berlinetta dashboard was also conserved, including the instrumentation and air vents. The trunk had the same capacity as the Berlinetta (11,288.7 cu. in. –185 liters), given the absence of the spare tire (replaced by the renowned crash-proof fire extinguisher). However, to improve the pleasure of a thrilling drive, there were small details such as the roll bars. The perforated pedal board, old-style tank cap and adjustable suspensions contributed to the illusion that one was really at the wheel of a racecar. Still in 2000, Pininfarina presented another car, the Rossa, destined only for the grand international motor shows.

216-217 and 218-219 The Barchetta Pininfarina was a good attempt at the reproduction of past models, those remarkable and thrilling "toys," for those who loved the pleasure of driving in the open air, ready to astound with its exclusive Formula One technological transfers.

Ferrari Enzo

Historic year

2004 will be remembered as an extraordinary year in the history of the Prancing Horse. Michael Schumacher and his F2002 demonstrated an almost embarrassing superiority: the German won 11 Grand Prix World Championships, whereas the others went to Barrichello. But also production – 4,015 cars, with 1,924 employees – brought about clamorous affirmations like those of the Enzo, so baptized in memory of its founder. The heir of the F50 and an extreme Grand Touring roadster, it was designed and built with the same care and attention as a Formula One car, but had to circulate on the road in all safety. And these were not just words of convenience: the Enzo was conceived to give the sensational emotions of 217 mph (350 km/h), on track, obviously. Single-seaters were tested, numbered (with specific plates on the dashboard) and 399 cars produced, selling at that time for 665,000 euros each. It was an extreme Grand Tourer defined in every detail, but each driver could adapt it to his own demands thanks to two adjustments (sports and race), to be effected with the corresponding adjustments of the dampers and the traction control (ASR). The entire project ended in 1998; it was the fruit of long aerodynamic and structural studies on the computer, as well as in track tests that always confirmed validity and safety. Its dimensions were not casual: it measured 15.41 ft. (4.7 m) long, over 6.56 ft. (2 m) wide and 3.6 ft. (1.1 m) high; these measurements were but natural for a car of this type. "It is an overview of the dynamics of the 1990s," said Engineer Lorenzo Ramaciotti (in those years under Pininfarina), head of the Enzo design. "As a descendent of the F1 of the 1990s, some aspects today should perhaps be revised, but the Enzo still remains innovative and functional thanks to its aerodynamics as the guiding principle of the design, to obtain greater vertical loads and, therefore, more grip without using eclectic and bulky flaps that would condition its line." Aerodynamics was the guiding force that improved all the components and performances of the F50, to which the car was heir, in its profiling, without turning to the now over-

220-221 and 222-223 This precious gem of 2000 was an object of desire, with only 399 units built and sold to clients all over the world. Aerodynamics was still the master of the Enzo project, which kept it gripped to the ground even at 186 mph (300 km/h).

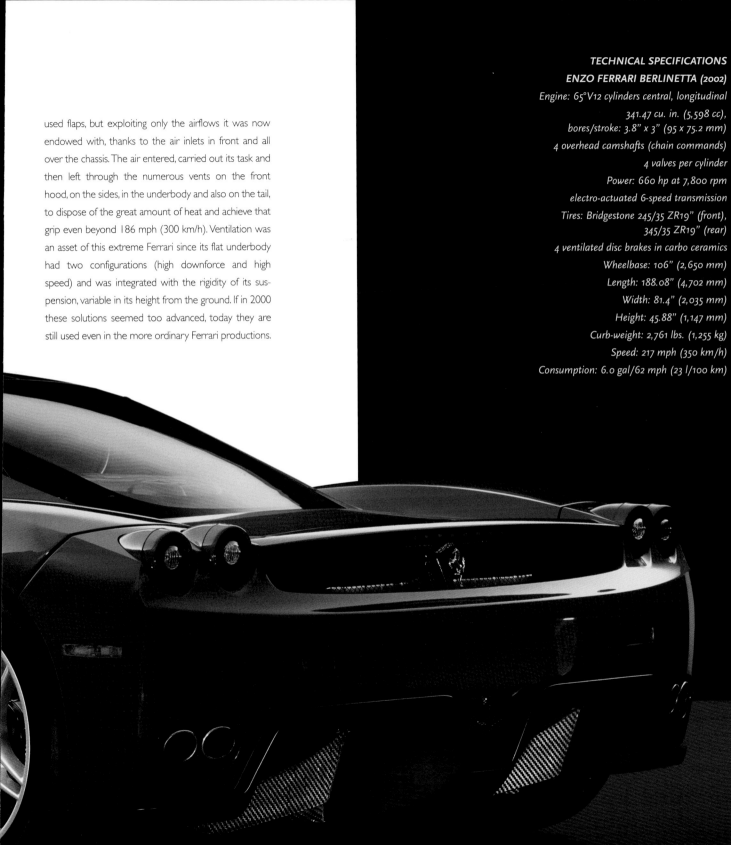

used flaps, but exploiting only the airflows it was now endowed with, thanks to the air inlets in front and all over the chassis. The air entered, carried out its task and then left through the numerous vents on the front hood, on the sides, in the underbody and also on the tail, to dispose of the great amount of heat and achieve that grip even beyond 186 mph (300 km/h). Ventilation was an asset of this extreme Ferrari since its flat underbody had two configurations (high downforce and high speed) and was integrated with the rigidity of its suspension, variable in its height from the ground. If in 2000 these solutions seemed too advanced, today they are still used even in the more ordinary Ferrari productions.

TECHNICAL SPECIFICATIONS
ENZO FERRARI BERLINETTA (2002)
Engine: 65°V12 cylinders central, longitudinal
341.47 cu. in. (5,598 cc),
bores/stroke: 3.8" x 3" (95 x 75.2 mm)
4 overhead camshafts (chain commands)
4 valves per cylinder
Power: 660 hp at 7,800 rpm
electro-actuated 6-speed transmission
Tires: Bridgestone 245/35 ZR19" (front),
345/35 ZR19" (rear)
4 ventilated disc brakes in carbo ceramics
Wheelbase: 106" (2,650 mm)
Length: 188.08" (4,702 mm)
Width: 81.4" (2,035 mm)
Height: 45.88" (1,147 mm)
Curb-weight: 2,761 lbs. (1,255 kg)
Speed: 217 mph (350 km/h)
Consumption: 6.0 gal/62 mph (23 l/100 km)

Driving as in Formula One!

The carbon fiber underbody weighing 202.4 lbs. (92 kg) guaranteed superior safety levels: this was demonstrated in the Formula One mishaps, where terrible accidents often resulted in serious trauma. The driver's seat, a technological combination of design and functionality, exploited all the benefits ensured by control electronics. The instruments were an analog and digital mix of the most important instruments, rev counter and odometer. The car possessed a digital display on the left for pressures, the temperature of the mechanics and the fuel level, as well as other commands for the lights, start-up and air-conditioning on the narrow, central console. The illusion of driving an F1 was complete. Air-conditioning was effective and driving stability had seats with the body in carbon fiber. Besides the central airbag there were two rays of steering wheel push-buttons to adjust the setting and exclude anti-skidding. The driver's seat, if not for anything else, was worth the astronomical cost of 665,000 euros for the progressive 6-speed transmission on the steering wheel, with two flaps. The seats with underbody in carbon fiber were designed to resist better on the faster bends. The driver's seat definitely responded to the requirements of the supercars of this type. The drive in itself, thanks to electronics, made a great leap forward to the benefit of the less expert drivers, who could drive (but not at redline limits) this good "monster" of 660 hp, which weighed 2,761 lbs. (1,255 kg). It hit unthinkable speeds (well over 186 mph (300 km/h), and offered lightning acceleration (registered at 0-62 mph – 100 km/h in 3.7 sec., 0-173.6 mph – 280 km/h in 23.3 sec.) that always had to be kept in mind, though with all the safety measures possible in the year 2000: great disc brakes in Carbo Ceramics, ABS and anti-skids, with a stopping distance and resistance to fatigue that were unthinkable years earlier.

224-225 The nose of the Enzo was almost intimidating, but carried out a fundamental task of directing the air flows in the underbody, radiators, crankshaft and brakes without using any aerodynamic supplements.

226-227 The tail offered numerous examples of evolved aerodynamics, such as air vents from the crankshaft and air venting ramps for ground effect, the integrated mobile flap and cabin profiling.

228-229 The sandwich panel chassis had wide, easy-access doors. The rear spoiler was mobile (stroke of 3 in. – 75 mm) from 0 to 155 mph (250 km /h).

230-231 Its profile confirmed the accurate research on chassis aerodynamics, targeting the best profiling-grip compromise: high nose with flap and tail in a negative lift profile.

227 top The Enzo mounted the historic but renovated 65° V12 cylinders. It was a 366.12-cu. in. (6-liter) engine branded F140 (225 kg) four valves per cylinder, Bosch fuel injection and dry sump lubrication. Also in full view were the horizontal dampers with variable calibration on three levels.

Ferrari F430

An extra designer

2004 was a very important year for the Prancing Horse with its F2004, and Michael Schumacher, who won almost all the Grand Prix for the season and the two world Drivers' and Constructors' titles. Things went well also for production, since 4,833 cars were made with two basic models: the 612 Scaglietti, in memory of the one who built the most sportive Ferrari cars, and the "tiny" F430, substitute for the 360 Modena. In the Grand Touring sector there were new heads in charge of the Ferrari line – once again the Pininfarina, but now with the support of Frank Stephenson of the Ferrari Style Center. The F430 took up the motifs of the F360 but transformed them according to the wishes of President Montezemolo, to achieve a totally different GT from the previous one and in line with the new aerodynamic trends. Its base benefitted from some suggestions carried over from the F1 winner and the new model, which tried to reconcile the various stylistic and technical demands, increasingly with the help of the wind tunnel. Once again the decision was to best exploit the air flows that hit the car above and under the bodywork, directing them with bigger air inlets and making them stream out through the numerous vents on the chassis. This defined the car's new configuration, though maintaining practically the same dimensions: wheelbase always at 8.52 ft. (2.6 m), length over 1.36 in. (3.5 cm), width and height unchanged, weight of weighing 132 lbs. (60 kg) more. The front had two big air inlets, always with the small central flap, which directed the incoming air flow better; the same concepts were repeated on the sides, with air inlets for the engine and brake shaft that did not upset the main soft lines of the sides.

232-233 The F430 took its cues from the 360 Modena of 1999: aerodynamic thrust, electronics at the maximum, and spine-chilling performance (over 195.3 mph or 315 km/h), 0-62 mph –100 km/h in 4 sec.). It was produced until the creation of the 458 Italia in 2009.

234-235 The F430's tail revealed all the aerodynamic tips carried over from the latest Ferraris, including grand rear ramps with four vertical louvers to vent the underbody's airflows.

TECHNICAL SPECIFICATIONS

F430 (2004–2007)

Engine: 90° V8 cylinders central longitudinal
262.78 cu. in. (4,308 cc),
bores/stroke: 3.68" x 3.24" (92 x 81 mm)
Bosch electronic injection
Power: 490 hp at 8,500 rpm
longitudinal and also progressive
6-speed transmission
Tires: 225/35 ZR 19" (front), 285/35 ZR 19" (rear)
Wheelbase: 104" (2,600 mm)
Curb-weight: 2,970 lbs. (1,350 kg)
Length: 180.48" (4,512 mm)
Width: 76.92" (1,923 mm)
Height: 48.56" (1,214 mm)
Speed: 184.6 mph (297.8 km/h)
Consumption: 4.76 gal/62 mi (18.3 l/100 km)

The rear was designed accurately with broader vents (also at the side of the rear window) and internal flows to improve aerodynamics, more efficient by 40 percent and with a downforce up to 286 lbs. (130 kg) greater than that of the F360. In short, also in this model the more important features came from the advanced study of aerodynamics, with a great rear slope that contributed to the improvement of the grip at high speeds and a maximum overall vertical load equivalent to 616 lbs. (280 kg).

The interior design did not move away from the setting of the 360 Modena, both in the dashboard and driver's seat. The concepts of the F360 were taken up, where analog and digital elements coexisted, besides the new "throttle lever" to define the behavior characteristics based on the driver's requests. It was possible to have the more racecar gear lever commands on the steering wheel, allowing for greater concentration at the wheel, or else the traditional ones with a central lever. The V8 of the F430 had a new structure

compared to the previous 360 Modena: engine displacement increased by 20 percent; output by 23 percent, hitting 490 hp; and torque by 25 percent. Besides other construction refinements, comprehensible in the artisanal dimensions of the very classy Ferrari cars, its dimensions were more compact, with new cylinder heads and four valves per cylinder (instead of five in the F360). The four camshafts were then chain-driven (instead of the toothed belt), with single-phased variable speed drive together with other refined items, to ensure better compensation. The transmission (longitudinal) with 6 speeds was still offered in two versions: electro-actuated gearbox with paddles on the steering wheel, or traditionally mechanical. Further subtleties were achieved in the mechanics to be transferred to road behavior: aluminum technology improved, and due to this, the chassis weighed 10 percent less and was more resistant to flexion and torsion, making the drive more precise and with greater comfort, and the driver benefitted from the ability to adjust the suspension. There was an ever-more-sophisticated electronics controlled output, along with torque, anti-lock ABS brakes, stability and traction control, brake corrector and the exclusive (E-Diff) self-locking differentials. These sophisticated, increasingly fast, and even comfortable Grand Tourers confirmed a more technological drive. The F430 would be replaced in 2007 by the 430 Scuderia, which would take up its characteristics and also upgrade its output to 510 hp.

236-237 and 238-239 The Spider was built in 2005 for open-air driving, hitting a top speed of 197.16 mph (318 km/h) in all safety with carboceramic brakes. The top was quickly mounted (in about 20 seconds) and had robust safety roll bars. Also on the Spider model, the crankshaft was in full view.

Ferrari 612 Scaglietti

Sit back and relax, even at almost 200 mph (300 km/h)

Even the Ferrari cars changed their characteristics: the 186 mph (300 km/h) no longer sufficed (the 612 even hit 198 mph – 320 km/h as clocked), but now even all the other refinements and amenities the category offered were indispensable for a fast, easy and safe drive. The "6" in the name stood for the engine displacement of 350.01 cu. in. (5,738 cc) and "12" was the number of the cylinders; the name Scaglietti paid homage to the legendary body designer. Once again it was driven by a 12-cylinder engine, here in fantastic condition with 540 hp, 98 more with respect to the outgoing 456 M of 1998, overhauling the engine and the entire chassis, though conserving the fundamental style lines of the trademark. The car was designed for comfortable traveling for four, and still being a Ferrari, it certainly could not renounce its prestigious sporty DNA profile. It was the fastest four-seater then, even if its wheelbase, compared to its predecessor, was increased by 1.95 in. (5 cm), essential to offering more room and greater comfort to passengers. In reality it

was supposed to be a more streamlined car with a coupe personality, a compartment moved back to the rear and a technology that exploited the best possibilities aluminum could offer. But the requirements for safety and comfort had increased throughout the years and due to this, the 612 weighed (curb weight) 4,048 lbs. (1,840 kg) more than Ferrari 456. Despite its dimensions, the line still possessed a Ferrari personality: long fenders, muscular sides, some edges, the clipped tail and above all the large side scallops (recalling the 1950s) visually lightened the mass of the coupe, which was 16.07 ft. (4.9 m) long and almost 6.56 ft. (2 m) wide.

The 612 Scaglietti offered greater comfort immediately when accessed, thanks to an opening joints system of the two wide doors and the arrangement of the seats that were electrically adjustable in various directions. The longitudinal space remained almost the same as that of the 456, but the furnishings and trimmed seats guaranteed more than adequate com-

fort for the passengers. The sumptuous finish in Connolly leather and an accurate assembly with more abundant padding at the contact points were assets for the 612. The driver benefitted most, and besides the gearshift paddles on the steering wheel, could avail himself of sensors that turned on the lights, a "rain shower" for the windshield wipers and parking. Also the trunk was 20 percent larger, now 1,464 cu. in. (240 liters). However, for this big, luxury Berlinetta, a broad range of Scaglietti catalogs allowed for customized 612 settings as needed, more comfortable or more sportive, with a carbon or 20-inch steering wheel and even a dual-toned chassis.

The scheme remained the same as in the previous 456 but along the 12 years that separated the two cars,

240-241 and 242-243 For fast, easy and comfortable driving, the 612 Scaglietti offered more room in the interior (+13.65 in. – 35 cm). With a smooth and pleasant aluminum chassis, it did not use aerodynamic flaps but had two hulls on the sides.

many things had been improved in the transaxle technology. In order to concentrate the masses, the front V12 engine was moved backward without compromising more spacious livability both in front and behind. The car also possessed a rear-axle transmission and command paddles on the steering wheel, which enhanced appreciation of the agile handling characteristics of the Ferrari, thanks to the bigger wheelbase and the new aluminum chassis. Aerodynamics predominated since all the main modifications improved both the profiling (therefore the Cx) and the downforce, thanks to its flat base for "ground effect" with a total of 253 lbs. (115 kg) for the vertical load (at 186 mph – 300 km/h), which maintained a stronger grip to the ground. The flat base produced a "blower" that not only disposed of the

heat produced by the mechanics, but when speeding, kept the rear axle gripped even more to the road. The distribution of weight was also important, with 46 percent on the front axle and the remaining 54 percent on the rear axle; it contributed to road handling with few surprises, plus a slight and pleasant oversteer in its behavior at bends. Electronics were always there to monitor such a great mass and superpower, controlling the suspension, swerves and brakes and avoiding sharp losses in grip, also thanks to the traction control (CST). This was, therefore, a coupe of great prestige, in the pursuit of maximum comfort and very high performance (it could surpass 198.4 mph – 320 km/h), and accelerate from 0 to 62 mph (100 km/h) in only 4.3 seconds. It feared no comparison to competitors.

TECHNICAL SPECIFICATIONS
612 SCAGLIETTI (2004)

Engine: 65° V12 cylinders

350.01 cu. in. (5,738 cc),
bores/stroke: 3.56" x 3.08" (89 x 77 mm)

Bosch electronic injection

Power: 540 hp at 7,250 rpm

4 overhead camshafts, 4 valves per cylinder

manual 6-speed transmission
electro-actuated rear-axle

Tires: 245/45 ZR 18" (front), 285/40 ZR 19" (rear)

Weight: 4,048 lbs. (1,840 kg)

Length: 196.08" (4,902 mm)

Width: 78.28" (1,957 mm)

Height: 53.76" (1,344 mm)

Speed: 195.3 mph (315 km/h)

Ferrari 458 Italia

Allow us to dream

"One last dream": this was how Ferrari, in a poetic impulse, unveiled the last compact model of the house. The numbers indicated the engine displacement (274.43 cu. in. – 4,499 cc) and the cylinders (8) of a mid-engine two-seater Berlinetta with a record-breaking output – one that should have exploited all the lessons learned from the races and especially from the Formula One (aerodynamics, engines, chassis, suspensions). The design once again was determined by aerodynamic performance and from the best integration between profiling, (coefficient Cx) and the downforce (Cz). As a matter of fact, the aerodynamics that dictated the development lines were immediately detectable because of the shape of the chassis: the numerous air inlets and the vents over the entire body, along with all the other motives, fruits of the research and experiences gathered from these components on this record-breaking Berlinetta. It was 14.76 ft. (4.5 m) long, 6.23 ft. (1.9 m) wide and 3.93 ft. (1.2 m) high – so, in the

same order of size as its predecessor, the F430. The car had a sharply different design from the previous models. Above all, the two great "mouths" on the front, which many disliked, were replaced by just one central inlet that captured all the air flows distributed through the mechanics, the flat base and the underbody, so as to obtain excellent results, with a Cx of 0.33 (even better than that of the F430) and a greater Cz, which meant greater grip of the ground. It was indeed a very interesting result.

Cooperation between Pininfarina and the Ferrari Styling Center continued with the indispensable support of the wind tunnel. What stood out was a dominant nose that captured the air flows counteracting the machine. Its narrow sides streamlined the design and the more "muscular" wheel housing, evidenced by tires of a good 20 inches. Along the entire chassis were slopes that better directed the air flow towards the rear – another dominant element of the chassis, with the inevitable disposal from the

flat base. It was a really exclusive design and very pleasant on the whole. If some solutions may have aroused doubt, they determined, according to one's tastes, a pleasant but certainly exclusive personality. The benefits acquired from many years of racing were evident in the perfect and almost aggressive layout of the various components, such as that of the front spoiler with air flow deviation functions, and the many air inlets (big and small) that determined the strong road-grip. They ensured excellent results even without exploiting the options offered by the great and flashy flaps; the 458 chassis re-

mained smooth, with softly connected surfaces.

Maranello had produced the 8-cylinder engine for over 35 years, but on the 458 it hit the limit levels (127 hp/liter), with engine torque essential to the transmission steadiness and progressions, 20 percent higher than the F430. In the conduits: all the V8 components were subjected to special treatments to reduce friction (the engine going at 9,000 revs) and direct injection, and diminish consumption, besides improving performance. Precisely since the times of the (Dino) V8, Maranello had developed a sound that the more passionate and competent Fer-

rari faithful loved. Also, the longitudinal transmission was overhauled, thanks to the progressive 7-speeds and dual clutch gears, which reduced the gearshift time, improving also the low speed run. There was even an E-Diff3 electronic differential, adequate for high performance. These improvements implied benefits also in safety and speed comfort, at levels which no one would have imagined a few years back. A series of handling modes established by the driver and the electronics facilitated the drive: a specific F1-Trac traction control accurately assessed the grip level, improving mobility even at high perform-

ance. A series of electronic procedures avoided errors or driving imperfections, but required swift technological reflexes and know-how – the instructions manual had to be read attentively – plus a good deal of training. Also the suspension was overwhelmed by the winds of change: the front axle was triangular in L-shape overlays, while the rear axle had a multilink scheme with multiple arms. The suspension was also electronically controlled (SCM) with a controlled damping factor as in the servo steer. The 20-inch tires took such super performance into account.

244-245 The 458 Italia evoked the traditions of the compact Ferraris with improvements in aerodynamics, technology and materials with 58 percent of its weight on the rear axle.

246-247 Designed for an exciting but safe drive, the nose of the 458 Italia revealed broad air inlets that selected the air flows.

TECHNICAL SPECIFICATIONS

458 ITALIA (2009)

Engine: 90° V8 cylinders central longitudinal
274.43 cu. in. (4,499 cc),
bores/stroke 3.76" x 3.24" (94 x 81 mm)
Bosch electronic injection
Power: 570 hp at 9,000 rpm
longitudinal gear with dual clutch and 7-speed transmission
Tires: 235/35 ZR 20 "(front), 295/35 ZR20" (rear)
Wheelbase: 104" (2,600 mm)
Length: 181.08" (4,527 mm)
Width: 77.48" (1,937 mm)
Height: 48.52" (1,213 mm)
Curb-weight: 3,036 lbs. (1,380 kg)
Speed: 201.5 mph (325 km/h)
Consumption: 3.45 gal/62 mi (13.3 l/100 km)

248-249 Careful studies were conducted on the tail to improve profiling but also on the downforce and grip thanks to a dynamic load of 616 lbs. (280 kg) on the car at 124 mph (200 km/h).

Ferrari California

Discovery of the California

Not by chance this name has appeared and reappeared in the Ferrari chronicles from the 1950s onward, given that today this prestigious Spider still exists, as a tribute to the splendid 1957 racecar and tourer that had always been the dream of young and old. Currently, however, unlike its splendid ancestor, the California presents itself not only as an attractive Pininfarina bodywork, but also one with a technological background not even conceivable over half a century ago. Back then, so much depended only on the extraordinary qualities of the mechanics of its 12-cylinder engine that enchanted sportsmen and royalty alike. The heart of the California 2011 was no longer the legendary 12 cylinders, but the new 8 cylinders, which occupied an important position among Ferrari's elite; it was Maranello's first front-mounted V8 engine, and this was also the first Spider of the house to mount an electrically controlled, metal convertible top. The bodywork, always by Pininfarina, about 14.76 ft. (4.5 m) long, was an unusual mix of old and new style lines, with a nose that recalled the Ferrari cars of old, and expressed the personality of the sports Spider, weighing 3,586 lbs. (1,630 kg) – 47 percent on the front, 53 percent on the rear. Air scoops and louvers on the nose and on the sides lightened the weight, making the car more brassy and pleasant. The rest of the components were a *summa* of more recent experiences and offered guided assistance under all aspects: from the modern electronic measures and the automated 7-speed transmissions, to mobility control, and the stop-start device, very useful to stop and start in particular traffic conditions. The F1 dual-clutch transmission equipped with an intelligent strategy in the automatic

250-251 and 252-253 A new convertible supercar with a dual personality, the California had a new chassis, suspension and discs in carboceramics. The foldable and removable top occupied only 6,102 cu. in. (100 liters) of the 20,746.8 cu. in. (340 liters) of the trunk.

gearshifts not only optimized the engaging of the gears but also reduced consumption, resulting in an easier drive and greater acceleration on curves. Furthermore, the dual clutch was another unique, distinctive feature which canceled the "idle shift time" when changing gears. In addition to these systems, there was the now renowned exclusive feature of the "hand paddles" with which the driver selected the various behavior modes: "comfort" for all circumstances and also on wet roads, given that it acted on the gears, suspension and dampers; and "sport" for maximum performance and stability in perfect grip situations. The C/ST push-button, instead, canceled all the electric functions except the ABS. Among the other components for greater safety, the California offered the CCM brakes in carbon ceramic material that canceled the brake *fading* phenomenon and its duration, important benefits for such powerful and fast cars. It was not the first time that Ferrari made use of aluminum even on the chassis, with great rigidity; also here, however, the latest experience with this metal was logically exploited, as evidenced in the bodywork and mechanics.

TECHNICAL SPECIFICATIONS

CALIFORNIA (2009)

Engine: 90° V8 cylinders
262.11 cu. in. (4,297 cc),
bores/stroke: 3.76" x 3.09" (94 x 77.4 mm)
4 valves per cylinder
direct injection
Power: 460 hp at 7,750 rpm
FL dual clutch 7-speed transmission manual
6-speed on the rear axle
Tires: 245/40 ZR 19" (front),
285/40 ZR19" (rear)
Length: 180" (4,562 mm)
Width: 75" (1,909 mm)
Height: 51.08" (1,277 mm)
Weight: 3,817 lbs. (1,735 kg)
Speed: 192.2 mph (310 km/h)

The California was not a technological Spider rich in advanced solutions, but it offered levels of excellence also in the internal finishing, with Connolly leather everywhere, creating a really pleasant and top-class environment where the analog instrumentation and the digital components reasonably coexist. Even the many controls for the various functions, as in the recent Ferrari cars, may have initially left everyone dumbfounded due to the quantity and position of the push-buttons, levers, keys and electric adjustments. It required a careful study of the instruction manual to operate with precision all the various indispensable functions that transformed the Ferrari driver into an electronic technician. The compartment also conformed to the technological refinements: besides the Connolly leather in all the visible parts, space was wisely exploited: the rear bench could be used as a small two-seater bench seating or as a luggage deposit. With the backrest tilted, a more spacious load counter was achieved, up to 20,746.8 cu. in. (340 liters) or 14,644.8 cu. in. (240 liters) with the top open. Once "instructed," the driver could, then and there, acquire notions of the handling, speed, consumption and possibly, functional problems, assisted by excellent air-conditioning, along with a vehicle telematic system, and for the first time, by a *touch screen*. It integrated the satellite navigator or the rear video cam, making this extraordinary Spider's drive even more challenging, without forgetting that it could reach 192.2 mph (310 km/h) and accelerate from 0 to 62 mph (100 km/h) in less than four seconds.

254 top and 254-255 The picture on top shows the V8 engine of 262.38 cu. in. (4.3 liters), direct injection with 460 hp. Elegant and streamlined, the California underscored its good Spider-coupe profiling, which could open the top and stack it in the trunk in just a few seconds.

256-257 The California was conceived with great attention on aerodynamics with Cx of 0.33, which was also enhanced by the rear flap.

Ferrari 599 GTO

All the races

TECHNICAL SPECIFICATIONS

599 GTO (2010)

Engine: 90° V8 cylinders front

365.93 cu. in. (5,999 cc),
bores/stroke: 3.68" x 3" (92 x 75.2 mm)

4 valves per cylinder

Bosch electronic injection

Power: 670 hp at 8,250 rpm

F1 gearbox at the rear axle

6-speed, dual clutch

Tires: 285/30 ZR 20"
(front), 315/35 ZR 20" (rear)

Length: 188.4" (4,710 mm)

Width: 78.48" (1,962 mm)

Height: 53.04" (1,326 mm)

Curb-weight: 3,289 lbs. (1,495 kg)

Speed: 207.7 mph (335 km/h)

The name GTO has been in the Ferrari iconograph for over 50 years now, a trademark of its competitive spirit which has never slackened since its birth.

The making of this latest GTO started with the 599 GTB of 2006, and maintained the same engine displacement – revised, upgraded (to 670 hp) and improved in every detail, courtesy of the latest technological transfers from the track as well as from the know-how handed down from the company's history. But then, with all the means technicians and engineers possess today, the transformation of Grand Tourers into high-powered racecars is not a problem, especially if the base is as excellent as that of the Ferrari. Undertaking to perfect a Grand Tourer implies a good knowledge of the points to be taken up, to be able to obtain the best performance and increase driving pleasure, even in its current situation, where super

performances are really difficult to exploit, except on racetracks. This GTO of our time is easily recognizable due to the air vents and inlets on the engine lid, along with many other subtleties, which in Formula One have the task of decisively improving performance, cutting weight to 220 lbs. (100 kg) – an important factor for an already sportive Berlinetta. For example, the front shield was broadened to fair in the wheels better, and also the sills under the doors were rounded off to diminish the loss of energy due to the turbulence of the wheels. Moreover, to ensure a stronger grip on the front, there was now a flap to augment the downforce – modifications that only apparently did not affect road behavior. To sum up, the 458 Italia wanted to demonstrate without the shadow of a doubt the competitive aspirations of its mechanics, starting with the engine, which could deliver from an initial 620 hp to 7,000 revs

and from 670 to 8,250 revs, with a limiter that triggered at 8,400. Also here, exploited technology was transferred from the races (as for the drive shaft), derived from research on cross induction pipes as well as on the metallurgy of components, useful also in diminishing consumption and emissions with the necessary modifications for adaptation to the road. The engine torque, in turn, offered a marked improvement from 608 to 620 Nm. The transmission conserves the basic transaxle philosophy, the V8 engine in front and the F1 gearbox at the rear, and the 6-speed F1 transmission. This reduced the overall time from declutching, disengaging and engaging the gears (60 milliseconds), making a more agile and immediate (by 20 percent) response even in the downshift progression of the gears with the command paddles now frequently used on the Ferrari models. The braking system pursues maximum performance, as in the stopping distances and resistance, thanks to the second generation CCM2 carbon ceramic system, much lighter and more powerful and less sensitive to hard usage. The development of the car control systems included the SCM2, the ESP (electronic stability control) for the suspension and the F1-Trac (traction control).

The interior is substantially that of the F599, even if the entire image has changed, giving it a decisive sportiness, with black as the dominant color, seats in technological material like corduroy fabric, various instrumentations and central dashboard with air-conditioning controls, redesigned in the sportive vision like all the upholstery of the seats and lateral paneling. The beautifully profiled wrap-around seats do not present problems even in more demanding driving; they elegantly combine luxury and sportiness – just think of the trims and floor in exposed aluminum which, when all is said and done, totally fulfill their tasks and justify such a high price: this is an extreme sports car which, however, offers the load capacity –19,526.4 cu. in. (320 liters) of an average Berlina and the 599 GTB.

We are not dealing here with mere appearance or the usual sports declarations: the GTO pays tribute to its ancestors in theory and on the track, since with 50 hp more compared to the original Berlinetta GTB, it shoots to a speed of over 207.7 mph (335 km/h) at 0 – 62 mph (0 – 100 km/h), achieved in an exceptional 3.35 seconds, and can reach 124 mph (200 km/h) in only 9.8 seconds. A particularly interesting note, perhaps more for technicians than for the Ferrari faithful: consumption in the mixed ECE cycle is 4.55 gal/62 mi. (17.5 l/100 km).

258-259 The GTO's nose immediately showed its aggressiveness carried over from racing technology with the negative lift hood, widened bumpers and faired-in wheels.

260-261 The aggressive nose of the 599 GTO pursued minimum weight to achieve a more precise driving. The thickness of the aluminum parts was reduced by 20 percent, glass panes were lighter, with carboceramic brakes and carbon structured seats.

Ferrari Four

262-263 A new style was born (Pininfarina-Ferrari). The forms were in continual motion in the Ferrari Four where a succession of edges, concavities and convexes together produced an outstanding effect. With a length of 16.07 ft. (4.9 mers) it had a V12 engine of 384.42 cu. in. (6.3 liters) with 660 hp and with molded flanks for greater efficiency with 20-inch wheels.

A perfect challenge

Maranello has launched a new challenge to the more qualified Grand Tourers of today and tomorrow – a sports car with truly innovative characteristics starting once again from the line designed by Pininfarina with Flavio Manzoni of the Ferrari Style Center, following the "shooting brake" settings – historically considered by the anglophones first as a "hunting carriage" and later as a fast station wagon for sports activities, calling to mind examples of the past, such as the Jensen FF of 1966-1971, the Beta HPE of 1975 or the BMW Z4 coupe of 2005. It stands out for its lines, a synthesis in fact between the station wagon and the coupe, but with the inevitably exclusive Ferrari mark. The car, called the FF, or rather the Ferrari Four, according to the house, boasts exceptional performances (over 207.7 mph – 335 km/h) and an acceleration from 0-62 mph (100 km/h) in just 3.7 seconds, with a record-making weight/output ratio of 5.94 lbs. (2.7 kg)/hp, but also offering the highest level of comfort. The flagship prototype, announced and displayed at the 2011 Geneva Motor Show, will be initially sold at an off-the-record price of 270,000 euros.

To start, the now consolidated Ferrari style lines, especially at the FF's nose, exhibit a great negative lift hood that points down to a very wide grille, with numerous air intakes and consequential supplementary air vents for the brakes, and a flat crankshaft and underbody for better grip at high speeds. With a length of 16.07 ft. (4.9 m), the FF is about 7.8 in. (20 cm) longer than the 599 GTO, and is the first and only modern station wagon produced by Maranello. A new concept of sportiness has been installed on this car, great output distributed on a four-wheel drive. The new 65° V12-cylinder engine, with direct injection deriving from the GTO engine, develops 660 hp that hurtles the FF to extreme performances despite its weight (3,938 lbs. – 1,790 kg) at 207.7 mph (335 km/h), also thanks to a type of aerodynamics that exalts exuberant output. Beside the very sporty Berlinetta performance, the car offers ample loading and customized possibilities, with an ever more spacious trunk (from 9,153 cu. in. – 150 liters to 48,816 cu. in. – 800 liters) and equipped with a rich set of accessories and efficient controls – proudly exhibiting its F1-Trac, the E-Diff and PTU (Power Transfer Unit) that transfers part of the torque onto the front wheels, anti-locking ABS, EBD and ESC. Its "clinical records" declare an ideal weight distribution of this kind, with a slight prevalence (53 percent) toward the rear – the most suitable for overtaking on fast bends.

4x4
by Maranello

TECHNICAL SPECIFICATIONS
FF (2011)

Engine: 65° V12 cylinders

381.98 cu. in. (6,262 cc),
bores/stroke: 3.76" x 3" (94 x 75.2 mm)

4 valves per cylinder

Bosch direct injection

Power: 660 hp at 8,000 rpm

all-wheel drive with F1 rear-wheel transmission,
7-speed dual clutch

carboceramic disc brakes

Tires: 245/30 ZR 20" (front), 295/35 ZR 20" (rear)

Length: 196.28" (4,907 mm)

Width: 78.12" (1,953 mm)

Height: 55.16" (1,379 mm)

Curb-weight: 3,938 lbs. (1,790 kg)

Speed: 207.7 mph (335 km/h)

The exclusive "all-wheel drive" designed at Ferrari's vaguely resembles the Porsche Panamera, remarkable for its light weight (about 50 percent less than the other "four-wheel drive" cars) and electronically handling every instant, the most suitable torque on every wheel. The independent wheel suspensions are of the Magnetorheological Damper (SCM2) type, already seen on the 599 GTO, with the indispensable support of the four-wheel drive that can transfer the 660 hp on all types of terrains, at low-grip roads or on the track, as evidenced by the performance beyond 207.7 mph (335 km/h) and a 0-62 mph (100 km/h) in 3.7 seconds. The

GTO of 670 hp, with two driving wheels and lighter than 649 lbs. (295 kg), takes two decimals less during the same tests. This very posh Ferrari costs much more than its direct competitors, such as the Panamera, and therefore cannot renounce its exclusive features, such as the direct-injection V12, here shown in its most brilliant form, set in the front at the height of the front wheels. There is a 7-speed gearbox on the rear wheel, with dual clutch driving the rear wheels and a four-wheel drive system that electronically handles the front driving wheels, so as not to exploit the entire, grand engine torque (683 Nm at 6,000 revs) in first or second gear. Also, the

chassis in light alloy – now a Ferrari custom – has been restructured for the new mechanics to ensure the necessary rigidity when running and leaving space for the all-wheel drive components. Other innovations are seen on the electronics and HELE system (High Emotion Low Emissions) that provides a Stop & Start technology with engine arrest in case of stop and go circumstances.

The interior displays the utmost levels, with four seats, the new dashboard and walls lined in very luxurious Frau leather, as well as an entertainment program in the back, with two screens for DVD, TV programs and HF system.

The FF has stepped into the great world of all-wheel drive systems with its own innovations, with which other existing 4 x 4s cannot compare. At most it may be said to resemble the Porsche Panamera, but it takes pride in its exclusive features, front engine and rear gearbox. Torque and output are in part transferred by the PTU (Power Transfer Unit) to the front-wheel drive only for that split instant needed to overcome low grip surfaces; electronic handling of the front driving wheels allows for the non-total exploitation of the grand engine (683 Nm at 6,000 revs) in first or second gear. The engine torque is handled

every instant on each wheel, since it depends on the control unit of all the dynamic controls (electronic differential E-Diff, traction control F1-Trac and torque transfer system PTU).

266-267 With minimum overhangs, surfaces molded with the air inlets and vents necessary for such typical "shooting brake" features, the underbody maintained ground grip and facilitated the lower air flows.

Author biography

ROBERTO BONETTO was born in Brussels on November 20, 1938, and became a freelance member of the editorial staff of the Italian automobile magazine "Quattroruote" in 1962 as he continued his studies at the Milan Polytechnic University. He became a professional journalist in 1965 and was employed full-time for said magazine as head of the automobile news and road trials sections, and later held the posts of vice editor, central editor and vice director. In the 1970s he worked with Architect Angelo Tito Anselmi on a book about the history of Italian automobile body designs, and wrote a volume for Sperling & Kupfer on "Rallies," translated in German by Motor Presse Verlag. In 2003/2004, following the "Ferrari Encyclopedia," he produced a big volume edited by RCS publisher on all the Ferrari activities from the 1930s to 2004. After he resigned from "Quattroruote-Domus" in 2004, he started working with "Gente Motori" reporting on car news – previews, services and driving tips – and then joined the De Agostini publishing house. He currently teaches at the Polytechnic School of Design and the Domus Academy, Milan.

Index

c = captions

1000 km Buenos Aires, 61
24 Hours Daytona, 128, 131
24 Hours Le Mans, 5c, 14, 16c, 18, 29, 36, 59c, 82, 87, 91, 104, 104c, 131
24 Hours Spa, 61
500 Miles Indianapolis, 16
6 Hours Watkins Glen, 131
9 Hours Kyalami, 131

A

Agnelli, Gianni, 14, 48c, 58, 61c, 154c, 218
Alboreto, Michele, 20, 158
Alesi, Jean, 20, 180, 184
Alfa Corse, 13, 29, 32
Alfa Romeo, 13, 13c, 14, 29, 32, 55, 58
Alfa Romeo 158 "Alfetta," 14, 29, 55
Alfa Romeo 159, 55
Alfa Romeo 1900, 48
Alfa Romeo 2500, 29
Alfa Romeo Giulietta Spider, 70
Alfa Romeo P2, 13c
Alfasud, 133
Alonso, Fernando, 22, 22c
Ascari, Alberto, 32, 32c, 55
Auto Avio Costruzioni 815, 30, 31, 32, 32c, 33

B

BAR, 22
Baracca, Francesco, 13
Bardot, Brigitte, 70
Barnard, John, 20, 170
Barrichello, Rubens, 222

Bellentani, Vittorio, 32
Berger, Gerhard, 20, 184
Bergman, Ingrid, 58
Bertone, 19, 39, 148
Bianchi Anderloni, Carlo Felice, 32
Biondetti, Clemente, 29
Bizzarrini, Giotto, 16, 22c, 87, 91, 90c
BMW Z4 Coupé, 265
Boano, 70, 83
Borzacchini, Mario Umberto Baconin, 32
Bracco, Giovanni, 82
Busso, Giuseppe, 13, 36

C

Campari, Giuseppe, 32
Campionato Francese della Montagna (French Mountain Championship), 131
Campionato Mondiale Marche, 90
Capelli, Ivan, 180
Carrera Panamericana (or Mexican) race, 48c, 55, 59c, 82
Centro Stile Ferrari (Ferrari Styling Center), 234, 246, 265
Chinetti, Luigi, 5c, 14, 16c, 36, 45, 55, 58, 70, 96, 104, 148
Chiti, Carlo, 87
Cisitalia, 29
Coburn, James, 70
Collins, Peter John, 16
Colombo, Gioacchino, 13, 14, 29, 36, 39, 50
Cooper Car Company, 16
Cooper, Gary, 16
Coppa d'Oro delle Dolomiti (Dolomites Cup), 50c
Coppa Intereuropa (Intra-European Cup), 48c
Cordero di Montezemolo, Luca, 184, 218, 234
Cortese, Franco, 14, 29

D

Del Monaco, Mario, 70
Dino, 16
Dusio, Piero, 29

E

Ellena, 83

F

Fangio, Juan Manuel, 16, 55
Fantuzzi, 106c
Ferrari 125 F1 (GPC), 29
Ferrari 125 Sport, 13, 14, 29, 32, 36
Ferrari 126 C, 143
Ferrari 126 C2, 20
Ferrari 126 C4, 158
Ferrari 1500 Sport, 13
Ferrari 166, 34, 35, 36, 38, 39, 40c, 48
Ferrari 166 Berlinetta, 40c
Ferrari 166 Inter Sport, 38, 38c, 39c
Ferrari 166 MM, 29, 40c
Ferrari 166 MM Sport Prototipo, 40c
Ferrari 166 MM Touring Barchetta, 14, 36, 39
Ferrari 166 SC, 14c, 36c
Ferrari 212 Export "Egg", 48
Ferrari 212 Export, 46, 47, 48, 48c, 49, 50, 50c, 52c
Ferrari 212 Inter, 14, 48, 48c, 49, 50, 52c
Ferrari 250 Europa, 58
Ferrari 250, 79
Ferrari 250 GT, 16, 48, 79, 82, 82c, 83, 84c, 87, 87c
Ferrari 250 GT 2+2, 16, 113
Ferrari 250 GT Berlinetta, 70
Ferrari 250 GT California, 5c, 68, 69, 70, 70c, 71, 75c
Ferrari 250 GT Europa, 82
Ferrari 250 GT Lusso, 16
Ferrari 250 GT SWB, 70, 75c, 80, 81, 82, 82c, 83, 84, 84c, 85, 86, 87, 87c, 91
Ferrari 250 GT "Tour de France," 83
Ferrari 250 GTO, 16, 22c, 79, 87, 88, 89, 90, 90c, 91, 91c, 94, 104, 113
Ferrari 250 Le Mans, 16, 102, 103, 104, 104c, 113
Ferrari 250 S, 82
Ferrari 250 Testarossa, 106c
Ferrari 275 Daytona, 16c

Ferrari 275 G.P., 29

Ferrari 275 GTB, 92, 93, 94, 95, 95c, 96, 101b, 113, 130, 181c

Ferrari 275 GTB/4, 94, 95, 96

Ferrari 275 GTS, 113

Ferrari 288 GTO, 145, 156, 157, 158, 159, 159c, 163, 163c, 164

Ferrari 288 GTO Biturbo, 20

Ferrari 308 GT4 "Dino", 148

Ferrari 308 GTB, 19, 133, 134, 135, 136, 158, 159

Ferrari 308 GTB Coupé 2+2, 137c

Ferrari 308 GTB Spider, 137c

Ferrari 310 B, 22

Ferrari 312 B, 18

Ferrari 312 B2, 19

Ferrari 312 PB, 19

Ferrari 312 T, 19

Ferrari 312 T2, 19

Ferrari 312 T4, 20, 21c

Ferrari 312 T5, 20

Ferrari 315 S, 11c

Ferrari 328 GTB, 58, 145, 171, 172c

Ferrari 330 GT 2+2, 110, 111, 112c, 113

Ferrari 330 GTC, 114, 115, 130,

Ferrari 330 GTS, 114

Ferrari 340 America, 14, 44, 45

Ferrari 342 America, 42, 43, 44, 45, 45c

Ferrari 348, 136, 145, 172, 184,

Ferrari 348 GTB, 184, 185, 186, 187

Ferrari 348 TB, 20, 168, 169, 170, 170c, 172c, 173

Ferrari 348 TS, 20, 168, 169, 170, 170c, 172c,

Ferrari 360 GT, 215

Ferrari 360 Modena, 22, 22c, 187, 206, 207, 208, 208c, 209, 211, 212, 213, 234, 234c, 236, 237

Ferrari 360 Modena Spider, 208, 211c,

Ferrari 365, 112c

Ferrari 365 Coupé, 18, 125

Ferrari 365 Daytona Spider, 130, 130c

Ferrari 365 GT 2+2, 18, 122, 123, 124, 124c, 125

Ferrari 365 GT/4, 125, 131

Ferrari 365 GT/4 2+2, 19, 180

Ferrari 365 GT/4 BB, 19, 140, 152, 152c, 190

Ferrari 365 GTB "Hunchback", 18

Ferrari 365 GTB/4 Daytona, 18, 79, 96, 125, 126, 127, 128, 129c, 204

Ferrari 365 P, 18

Ferrari 365 Spider, 18,

Ferrari 375, 16, 58,

Ferrari 375 America, 56, 57, 58, 58c, 59c, 60, 61, 61c, 82

Ferrari 375 MM, 58, 58c, 59c, 61, 63c

Ferrari 375 MM Berlinetta Pininfarina, 59c, 65c

Ferrari 375 Plus, 58c, 61

Ferrari 375 Plus Barchetta, 59c

Ferrari 375 Plus Spider, 58

Ferrari 400 GT, 180

Ferrari 400 GTA, 19

Ferrari 400 Superamerica (SA), 106c, 114

Ferrari 400, 125

Ferrari 410 Superfast, 16, 58

Ferrari 412, 125, 145, 180, 181

Ferrari 412 T1, 184

Ferrari 430 Scuderia, 237

Ferrari 456 GT, 20, 148, 178, 179, 180, 181, 181c

Ferrari 456 M, 242

Ferrari 456 M Coupé 2+2, 177

Ferrari 458 Italia, 22, 234c, 244, 245, 246, 247, 247c, 249, 249c

Ferrari 500 Barchetta, 22

Ferrari 500 BB, 20

Ferrari 500 Superfast, 113

Ferrari 512 BB, 138, 139, 140, 141c, 143, 143c

Ferrari 512 BBi, 140, 143

Ferrari 512 M Spider, 191

Ferrari 512 TR (Testarossa), 145, 152

Ferrari 550 Barchetta Pininfarina, 215, 216, 217, 218, 219, 219c

Ferrari 550 Maranello, 22, 143, 154, 177, 191c, 202, 203, 204, 205, 205c, 218, 219

Ferrari 575 M Maranello, 22, 204, 215

Ferrari 599 GTB Fiorano, 22, 215, 260, 261

Ferrari 599 GTO, 258, 259, 260, 261, 261c, 265, 266

Ferrari 612 Scaglietti, 22, 181c, 215, 234, 240, 241, 242, 242c, 243

Ferrari 641 F1, 21c

Ferrari BB, 133

Ferrari California, 22, 250, 251, 252, 252c, 253, 255, 255c

Ferrari Challenge, 172

Ferrari Dino 206 GT, 79, 116, 117, 118, 118c, 120, 120c, 121, 136

Ferrari Dino GT, 18, 19, 58

Ferrari-Enzo, 22, 199, 215, 220, 221, 222, 222c, 223, 224, 224c, 226c, 227c

Ferrari-Enzo FXX, 215

Ferrari F1-87, 20

Ferrari F1-89, 20

Ferrari F2002, 222

Ferrari F2003-GA, 22

Ferrari F2004, 234

Ferrari F2007, 215

Ferrari F355, 20, 170, 177, 182, 183, 184, 185, 185c, 186, 187, 208, 208c, 213

Ferrari F355 F1, 22, 177

Ferrari F355 GTS, 185

Ferrari F355 Spider, 177, 185c, 186c

Ferrari F399, 208

Ferrari F40, 20, 145, 158, 159, 160, 161, 163, 163c, 164, 164c, 165, 167c, 170

Ferrari F430, 22, 22c, 213, 215, 232, 233, 234, 234c, 236, 237, 246, 247

Ferrari F430 Spider, 237c

Ferrari F50, 11c, 20, 177, 192, 193, 194, 195, 195c, 196, 197c, 198, 199, 199c, 222

Ferrari F512 M (Testarossa), 152, 188, 189, 190, 191, 191c

Ferrari F92 A, 180

Ferrari Four, 262, 263, 264c, 265, 265c, 266, 267, 267c

Ferrari GT Mondial, 20, 58,

Ferrari GTB Turbo, 145

Ferrari GTB V6, 20

Ferrari Mondial 8, 145, 146, 147, 148, 148c, 149

Ferrari Mondial T, 145, 148, 170

Ferrari Mythos, 20, 194

Ferrari Rossa Pininfarina, 219

Ferrari Superamerica, 22

Ferrari Superamerica Spider, 215

Ferrari Testarossa, 20, 58, 92, 106c, 143, 145, 150, 151, 152 152c, 154, 154c, 155, 158, 170, 172c, 190, 191c

Ferrari Testarossa Spider, 154c

Ferrari TRI 330 Le Mans, 5c, 102, 103, 104c, 106c, 107

Ferrari, Alfredo, 136

Ferrari, Enzo, 5c, 13, 13c, 14, 16, 16c, 20, 21c, 29, 32, 36, 45, 55, 58, 70, 90, 114, 118, 124, 144, 145, 148, 158, 163, 163c, 170

Fiat, 16, 18, 29, 32c, 48, 79, 118, 118c, 133, 145

Fiat 127, 133

Fiat 128, 133

Fiat 1400, 48

Fiat 500, 70, 79, 87

Fiat 500 "Mouse," 29

Fiat 500 B, 48

Fiat 500 C, 55

Fiat 508 C, 32

Fiat 600, 87

Fiat 850, 113

Fontana, 48

Ford, 18, 63c, 94

Forghieri, Mauro, 16, 87, 91

Frankfurt Motor Show, 130

Fusaro, Piero, 184

G

Gendebien, Olivier, 83, 104c, 154c
Geneva Motor Show, 40c, 265
Ghia, 39, 45, 48, 63c
Giro di Sicilia (Tour of Sicily), 29, 36, 50
Guichet, Jean, 83

H

Häkkinen, Mika, 22
Hamilton, Lewis, 22
Hawthorn, Mike, 16, 48,
Hill, Graham, 87
Hill, Phil, 104c

J

Jensen FF, 265

K

Kamm, Wunibald, 90, 94

L

Lamborghini, 94
Lamborghini Jarama, 133
Lamborghini Miura, 128
Lampredi, Aurelio, 39, 45, 61
Lancia, 29, 55
Lancia 2000, 133
Lancia Aurelia, 48
Lancia Aurelia B24, 70
Lancia Beta HPE, 265
Lancia Fulvia, 133
Lancia LC2, 158
Lauda, Niki, 19
Leopold III, King of Belgium, 45, 45c
Lotus, 16, 18

M

Magnum P.I., 137c
Mairesse, Willy, 83, 87
Mansell, Nigel, 20
Manzoni, Flavio, 265
Marzotto, Umberto, 50c
Marzotto, Vittorio, 48, 50

Maserati, 94
Maserati 250F, 16
Massa, Felipe, 22
Massimino, Alberto, 32
Materazzi, Nicola, 158
McLaren-Honda, 20
McLaren-Mercedes, 22
McLaren-Porsche, 20
Meazza, Stefano, 48c
Mercedes, 16, 82
Mille Miglia, 11c, 14, 14c, 29, 32, 36, 45, 45c, 50, 55, 82, 218
Monza Circuit, 13c, 48c
Moss, Stirling, 87
Motor Trend, 148
Munaron, Gino, 36
Murray, John, 82c

N

Navone, Giuseppe, 29
Nuvolari, Tazio, 14c, 29, 36c

P

Paris Motor Show, 82, 95, 96c, 136, 152
Parkes, Mike, 87
Pavesi, 191
Perón, Juan Domingo, 45, 48, 48c
Pescara, circuit, 32
Piacenza Circuit, 13, 29
Pininfarina (Pinin Farina), 14, 16, 18, 19, 20, 39, 45, 45c, 48, 58, 58c, 59c, 60c, 65c, 70, 70c, 82, 82c, 83, 87, 91, 94, 104, 112c, 113, 118, 128, 136, 140, 143, 148, 148c, 152, 163, 163c, 170, 170c, 181c, 185, 190, 191, 191c, 194, 204, 205c, 216, 218, 219, 222, 234, 246, 252, 264c, 265
Pironi, Didier, 20
Porsche, 18, 94, 95, 96
Porsche 911S, 118, 120, 120c
Porsche 917, 18
Porsche Panamera, 266, 267
Prost, Alain, 20, 21c

R

Räikkönen, Kimi, 22, 215
Ramaciotti, Lorenzo, 180, 218, 222

Rangoni Machiavelli Lotario, marquise, 32, 32c
Razelli, Giovanni Battista, 145
Red Bull-Renault, 22
Regazzoni, Clay, 19
Renault, 22
Renault 5, 133
Rethy, Lilian, princess of, 48, 112c
Reutemann, Carlos, 143
Righini family, 32
Rodriguez brothers, 87

S

Sagan, Françoise, 70
Scaglietti, 5c, 16, 70, 70c, 82c, 83, 87, 90c, 96, 104, 118, 128, 136, 152, 170, 185, 190, 191c, 242, 242c
Scheckter, Jody, 20, 21c
Schumacher, Michael, 22, 177, 198, 204, 208, 214, 215, 222, 234
Selleck, Tom, 137c
Selsdon, Peter, Lord 36
Senna, Ayrton, 20, 21c
Simca, 79
Stephenson, Frank, 234
Surtees, John, 16

T

Targa Florio, 91
Tour de France, 91, 131
Touring, 14, 32, 32c, 36, 39, 40c, 45, 48, 70
Trieste-Workshop 50c
Trips, Wolfgang von, 70
Turin International Motor Show, 36, 45

V

Vadim, Roger, 70
Vettel, Sebastian, 22
Vignale, 14, 39, 45, 45c, 48, 48c, 50c, 52c, 58, 70
Villeneuve, Gilles, 20, 21c
Villoresi, Gigi, 45, 48c
Volpi di Misurata, Count Giovanni, 70

W

Williams-Renault, 20

Aknowledgements

The Editor wishes to thank: Joanne Marshall, Ferrari S.p.A. Products Communications Director - Press Release Office

Photographic credits

Page 3 www.carphoto.co.uk

Pages 4-5 Fotostudio Zumbrunn

Pages 6-7 Fotostudio Zumbrunn

Pages 8-9 Fotostudio Zumbrunn

Pages 10-11 Pietro Carrieri/Tips Images

Pages12-13 Bettmann/Corbis

Pages 14-15 Fotostudio Zumbrunn

Page 17 Evening Standard/Getty Images

Pages 18-19 Fotostudio Zumbrunn

Page 20 Pascal Rondeau/Getty Images

Pages 20-21 Ron Kimball/KimballStock

Page 23 Clive Mason/Getty Images

Pages 24-25 Don Heiny/Corbis:

Pages 26-27 Ron Kimball/KimballStock

Page 28 center Fotostudio Zumbrunn

Page 28 right Ron Kimball/KimballStock

Page 28 left Ron Kimball/KimballStock

Pages 30-31 Giancarlo Reggiani

Pages 32-33 Giancarlo Reggiani

Pages 34-35 Fotostudio Zumbrunn

Page 37 Fotostudio Zumbrunn

Page 38 Fotostudio Zumbrunn

Pages 38-39 Fotostudio Zumbrunn

Pages 40-41 Ron Kimball/KimballStock

Page 41 LaPresse Archivio Storico

Pages 42-43 Fotostudio Zumbrunn

Page 44 LaPresse Archivio Storico

Pages 44-45 Fotostudio Zumbrunn

Pages 46-47 Fotostudio Zumbrunn

Page 48 LaPresse Archivio Storico

Pages 48-49 Fotostudio Zumbrunn

Page 50 Fotostudio Zumbrunn

Page 51 Fotostudio Zumbrunn

Pages 52-53 Ron Kimball/KimballStock

Page 54 right Fotostudio Zumbrunn

Page 54 center Fotostudio Zumbrunn

Page 54 left Fotostudio Zumbrunn

Pages 56-57 Fotostudio Zumbrunn

Page 58 LaPresse Archivio Storico

Pages 58-59 Fotostudio Zumbrunn

Page 60 Fotostudio Zumbrunn

Pages 60-61 Fotostudio Zumbrunn

Page 62 Fotostudio Zumbrunn

Pages 62-63 Fotostudio Zumbrunn

Pages 64-65 Fotostudio Zumbrunn

Pages 66-67 Fotostudio Zumbrunn

Pages 68-69 Fotostudio Zumbrunn

Pages 70-71 Fotostudio Zumbrunn

Pages 72-73 Fotostudio Zumbrunn

Pages 74-75 Fotostudio Zumbrunn

Page 78 right www.carphoto.co.uk

Page 78 left Fotostudio Zumbrunn

Page 78 center Fotostudio Zumbrunn

Pages 80-81 Fotostudio Zumbrunn

Pages 82-83 Fotostudio Zumbrunn

Page 84 Fotostudio Zumbrunn

Page 85 Fotostudio Zumbrunn

Page 86 Fotostudio Zumbrunn

Pages 88-89 Ron Kimball/KimballStock

Pages 90-91 www.carphoto.co.uk

Pages 92-93 Ron Kimball/KimballStock

Pages 94-95 Fotostudio Zumbrunn

Pages 96-97 Fotostudio Zumbrunn

Page 97 Fotostudio Zumbrunn

Pages 98-99 www.carphoto.co.uk

Pages 100-101 Fotostudio Zumbrunn

Pages 102-103 www.carphoto.co.uk

Pages 104-105 www.carphoto.co.uk

Page 105 www.carphoto.co.uk

Page 106 www.carphoto.co.uk

Page 107 www.carphoto.co.uk

Pages 108-109 www.carphoto.co.uk

Pages 110-111 Fotostudio Zumbrunn

Pages 112-113 Fotostudio Zumbrunn

Pages 114-115 Fotostudio Zumbrunn

Pages 116-117 Fotostudio Zumbrunn

Pages 118-119 Fotostudio Zumbrunn

Pages 120-121 Fotostudio Zumbrunn

Pages 122-123 Ron Kimball/KimballStock

Pages 124-125 Fotostudio Zumbrunn

Pages 126-127 Ron Kimball/KimballStock

Pages 128-129 Fotostudio Zumbrunn

Pages 130-131 Fotostudio Zumbrunn

Page 131 www.carphoto.co.uk

Page 132 right Fotostudio Zumbrunn

Page 132 center Fotostudio Zumbrunn

Page 132 left Ron Kimball/KimballStock

Pages 134-135 Ron Kimball/KimballStock

Page 136 www.carphoto.co.uk

Page137 Rue Des Archives/RDA

Pages 138-139 Fotostudio Zumbrunn

Pages 140-141 Fotostudio Zumbrunn

Pages 142-143 Fotostudio Zumbrunn

Page 144 right Fotostudio Zumbrunn

Page 144 center Ron Kimball/KimballStock

Pages 146-147 www.carphoto.co.uk

Pages 148-149 www.carphoto.co.uk

Pages 150-151 Fotostudio Zumbrunn

Pages 152-153 Fotostudio Zumbrunn

Page 153 Fotostudio Zumbrunn

Pages 154-155 Ron Kimball/KimballStock

Pages 156-157 Ron Kimball/KimballStock

Pages 158-159 Ron Kimball/KimballStock

Page 159 Ron Kimball/KimballStock

Pages 160-161 Ron Kimball/KimballStock

Pages 162-163 Ron Kimball/KimballStock

Pages 164-165 Fotostudio Zumbrunn

Pages 166-167 www.carphoto.co.uk

Pages 168-169 Ron Kimball/KimballStock

Pages 170-171 Fotostudio Zumbrunn

Pages 172-173 Fotostudio Zumbrunn

Pages 174-175 Fotostudio Zumbrunn

Page 176 center www.carphoto.co.uk

Page 176 left Ron Kimball/KimballStock

Page 176 right Ron Kimball/KimballStock

Pages 178-179 Ron Kimball/KimballStock

Pages 180-181 Ron Kimball/KimballStock

Pages 182-183 Ron Kimball/KimballStock

Pages 184-185 Ron Kimball/KimballStock

Pages 186-187 Ron Kimball/KimballStock

Pages 188-189 Ron Kimball/KimballStock

Pages 190-191 Ron Kimball/KimballStock

Pages 192-193 Fotostudio Zumbrunn

Pages 194-195 Fotostudio Zumbrunn

Page 196 Fotostudio Zumbrunn

Page 197 Fotostudio Zumbrunn

Pages 198-199 Ron Kimball/KimballStock

Pages 200-201 www.carphoto.co.uk

Pages 202-203 Ron Kimball/KimballStock

Pages 204-205 www.carphoto.co.uk

Pages 206-207 Ron Kimball/KimballStock

Pages 208-209 Ron Kimball/KimballStock

Pages 210-211 Ron Kimball/KimballStock

Pages 212-213 Ron Kimball/KimballStock

Page 214 center Ron Kimball/KimballStock

Page 214 right Ron Kimball/KimballStock

Page 214 left Fotostudio Zumbrunn

Pages 216-217 Ron Kimball/KimballStock

Pages 218-219 Ron Kimball/KimballStock

Pages 220-221 Fotostudio Zumbrunn

Pages 222-223 Fotostudio Zumbrunn

Pages 224-225 Fotostudio Zumbrunn

Pages 226-227 Fotostudio Zumbrunn

Page 227 Fotostudio Zumbrunn

Pages 228-229 Fotostudio Zumbrunn

Pages 230-231 Fotostudio Zumbrunn

Pages 232-233 Ron Kimball/KimballStock

Pages 234-235 Ron Kimball/KimballStock

Pages 236-237 Ron Kimball/KimballStock

Pages 238-239 Ron Kimball/KimballStock

Pages 240-241 Ron Kimball/KimballStock

Pages 242-243 Ron Kimball/KimballStock

Pages 244-245 Ron Kimball/KimballStock

Pages 246-247 Ron Kimball/KimballStock

Pages 248-249 Ron Kimball/KimballStock

Pages 250-251 Ron Kimball/KimballStock

Pages 252-253 Ron Kimball/KimballStock

Page 254 www.carphoto.co.uk

Pages 254-255 Ron Kimball/KimballStock

Pages 256-257 Ron Kimball/KimballStock

Pages 258-259 Ron Kimball/KimballStock

Pages 260-261 Ron Kimball/KimballStock

Pages 262-263 Ferrari S.p.A

Pages 264-265 Ferrari S.p.A

Page 265 Ferrari S.p.A

Pages 266-267 Ferrari S.p.A

Cover

2011 Ferrari 599 GTO.

© Ron Kimball/KimballStock

FERRARI

An Italian Legend

METRO BOOKS
New York

An Imprint of Sterling Publishing
387 Park Avenue South
New York, NY 10016

METRO BOOKS and the distinctive Metro Books logo are trademarks
of Sterling Publishing Co., Inc.

© 2011 by Edizioni White Star s.r.l.

This 2013 edition published by Metro Books,
by arrangement with Edizioni White Star s.r.l.

Translation: Yolanda Rillorta
Editing: Suzanne Smither

ISBN 978-1-4351-4580-1

For information about custom editions, special sales, and premium
and corporate purchases, please contact Sterling Special Sales at
800-805-5489 or specialsales@sterlingpublishing.com.

Manufactured in China

2 4 6 8 10 9 7 5 3 1

www.sterlingpublishing.com